TABLE OF CONTENTS

Introduction

This book is the continuation of the series; with the first book being the signs of the Judgement Day. In the previous book, we have talked about the major and signs the minor signs. We talked about all of the issues up until the coming of the Dajjal and the coming of Isa Ibn Maryam AS and Ya'juj and Ma'juj. Then we mentioned all signs until the Trumpet is blown.

Now, we will continue from where we left off. We're going chronologically This book begins the next section of this series. Which is going to be a very, very detailed discussion of this topic, that will turn to the Quran and Sunnah. And we'll discuss what we know about one of the most fundamental pillars of our religion. That is the Day of Judgement itself.

Day of Judgement, in fact, is one of the fundamental pillars that this whole religion is based upon. The three pillars are belief in Allah SWT, belief in the Prophet AS and belief in Judgement Day. These are the three fundamentals of all fundamentals.

So, we begin our discussion about the reality of Qiyamah. And we'll discuss what we know about Qiyamah. And what Allah SWT has mentioned of it, from the beginning of Qiyamah. Meaning the Trumpet being blown. Up until the very end, which is when people will be taken to their final destination.

Either Jannah, may Allah SWT make us amongst them. Or Jahannam, we seek Allah SWT's refuge from that. Then when we finish this part of our discussion, then after that we will begin a discussion of the two Dar ul Akhira; either Jannah, may Allah SWT make us amongst them, or description of Jahannam, so that we can be aware of it.

So, this will be the second book in series about the Qiyamah. And we will begin with an introduction to the concept of Qiyamah. And what Allah SWT mentions with regards to it. And how Allah SWT proves it. And what are the benefits of believing in Qiyamah.

Concept of Qiyamah

Of, course we realize that's belief in Qiyamah is not only a fundamental of our faith. It is a fundamental of all the Abrahamic faiths. It is something that marks The Abrahamic faiths from the non-Abrahamic faiths. Because all of the religions of the world are divided into two primary categories, the Abrahamic and then the dharmic religions.

These two put together form the bulk of the world religions. Anything outside of these two is very incidental or small. The Abrahamic religions are Judaism, Christianity and Islam. And put together these three faith traditions are more than half of the world's religions. The other major religions of the world are Hinduism and then of course Buddhism.

These are the two big religions other than ours. And then we have Jainism, to a smaller level. And then you have the Far Eastern religions like Shintoism. These are called the Dharmic religions. And the Dharmic religion share some things in common, just like the Abrahamic religions share some things in common.

Of the fundamentals of all Abrahamic religions is belief in the God of Abraham, and belief in the concept of Prophets AS, and belief in Judgement Day. These three are shared by all Abrahamic faith traditions. The

Dharmic religions don't believe in any of these things. And the concept of Judgment Day does not exist amongst all of them.

Now, what is the equivalent in all dharmic religions to judgement day? It is Reincarnation. Or the concept of liberation of the soul from the body. So, the goal of those faiths and religions is to break free from the cycle of reincarnation. In other words, achieve Nirvana or Moksha. The point is that they don't believe in a day of judgment. But those faiths do believe in some type of judgement. Because that's the whole point of Karma or reincarnation.

Even those faith traditions have some kernel of judgment. But it's not one judgment day. It is every soul shall have its own judgment. And then the resurrection of the next will be based upon what it has done. So, the point being that at some level, judgment is universal to all faith traditions of this world. Except that the Abrahamic faiths believe in one day, that is the day of Hisab, the day of Resurrection, the day of Qiyamah.

Now in Abrahamic faith traditions, all major sects of Christianity, and all mainstream groups of Islam; all of them believe in an Akhirah. Interestingly enough, for reasons beyond the scope this book, the Jewish faith tradition has veered from this belief. Once upon a time, classical Judaism, early Judaism, did believe in Qiyamah.

And Allah SWT references in the Quran that, they did believe in heaven and hell. However, over the course of the evolution of Jewish theology, slowly but surely, this concept, although if it was not fully discarded, but it is no longer central to the belief of most modern Jews.

Some still believe in it. And many have abandoned it. And most of them are agnostic about it. They don't know if it is possible or not. Even the religious and the practicing amongst them, have something that is now by and large, not mainstream amongst them. And It is very interesting to have abandoned this disbelief.

Now, when we look at Quran, belief in Qiyamah is one of the most fundamental principles of the entire religion. Some of our Scholars have said, and there is an element of truth to this, that you cannot read a single page of the Quran except that Allah SWT explicitly references to Qiyamah on it. There's definitely an element of truth that, you cannot read a single page of the Quran, except that there is an indirect or direct reference to the Qiyamah.

Rational Argument to Prove Qiyamah

Now, one of the interesting things about the concept of the Qiyamah is that, Allah SWT argues in the Quran with those who deny Qiyamah. Allah SWT reasons with them. He uses rational argument. He's essentially trying to prove Qiyamah in many different ways.

So, we begin our discussion about Qiyamah, by looking at some of the primary techniques that Allah SWT uses in the Quran to prove that the Qiyamah exists. And it's interesting that Allah SWT is using rational arguments here. Some people believe rationality has no role in the religion. And this is not true.

Allah SWT is using logical arguments. He's telling people who reject the Qiyamah to think that there is a Qiyamah. And he reasons with them in a logical manner. In a manner that he's trying to prove. And this is because the Quraysh generally speaking rejected the Qiyamah. The Quraysh didn't believe in Qiyamah.

They believed in Allah SWT. But they didn't believe in Prophets AS. And they didn't believe in Qiyamah. So, they rejected the two of the main three pillars of Islam. So, the Quran proves Prophets AS in many ways. But more than the Prophet AS, Quran proves the Qiyamah.

Because the Qiyamah is discussed more than triple the number of Prophets AS being discussed.

More than the Prophets AS, Allah SWT mentions the Qiyamah and attempts to prove its existence to the people who rejected it.

So, we will discuss seven specific techniques that the Quran uses to prove Qiyamah. And this is also a summary of a very good book in Arabic. A very large book, about how Allah SWT proves the Qiyamah in Quran. So, this is a summary and I have chosen 7 of the arguments.

Each one of these arguments is a genre, and under them are hundreds of versus. So, every point has a hundred examples. Not one or two examples, but hundreds of examples.

A Command of Allah SWT

The first genre of evidence, the first technique that Allah SWT uses is simply to say that, it is true. So, this is not rational as much as it is Allah SWT saying, "You need to believe in it because I'm saying so".

And of course, this is the bulk of the versus. Allah SWT says in Surah Fatiha, the first Surah of the Quran in the second verse, "I am the master of Judgment Day"; or "The Lord of Judgment Day". This is a statement of fact. Allah SWT is mentioning.

Included in this are **thousands** of verses that describe the Qiyamah. The majority of verses of Juz Amma are about Qiyamah. So, the bulk of all of these small Surahs, many of the verses of the Makkan Era, Allah SWT is describing Qiyamah. Allah SWT says in Quran, "When families will be split up", as a description of day of Qiyamah.

So, this comes under the first genres that Allah SWT is telling is that the Qiyamah is going to happen, and Allah SWT is describing how it will look like. And of these versus Allah SWT says in the Quran, "They ask you, is the Judgment Day really true". Then Allah SWT says one of the most powerful emphases in the Quran, "Say, **indeed** by my Lord, verily it is true". This is one of the most emphatic Verses in the Quran about Qiyamah.

Allah SWT is emphasizing in all seven ways, over and over again. Allah SWT is using words, **"Say"**; **"verily"**; **"I tell on to you"**; **"emphasizing it is true"**. So, the first genre is basically to say that it is happening and to describe what will be happening. This is not reasoning. This is simply telling us, 'It's going to happen. if you believe in me, then believe in this'.

Origin of Mankind

The second genre, which is a common motif of the Quran, where Allah SWT tells mankind to think about their own origin. And in thinking about our own origin, Allah SWT is saying, "Don't you think, I can bring your origin and do it all over again?"

Meaning, 'The one who created you for the first time, can he not recreate you again?' So, this is a logical reasoning. Basically, Allah SWT is saying, 'Why are you surprised that I can Resurrect the dead? Didn't I create you from nothing?'

So, there are again hundreds of verses in the Quran about this genre and this evidence. Allah SWT says in the Quran, "Doesn't mankind see where he comes from?" When Allah SWT describes where we came from, and Allah SWT describes the process of the evolution of the embryo, then Allah SWT says, "Don't you think I can do this all over again and bring you back?"

This is a direct rational appeal, that the one who created you in this manner, can recreate you again. And in the end of Surah Yasin Allah SWT says, "Doesn't mankind see that we created him from a drop of fluid, and lo and behold we created him from this fluid. Now, he is arguing with us".

What are we arguing about? Go back to the Seerah. Umayyah ibn Khalaf came to the Prophet SAW. He had in his hands a bone from an animal and he crumbled it. And he said, "Ya Muhammad SAW, do you think Allah SWT will bring this bone back to life when it has decayed?"

So, Allah SWT answered him by revealing the end of Surah Yasin. And it is such a powerful answer. Allah SWT says, "This man who is arguing with us, that whether we can bring life back or not, where did he come from? Now that he is Khasimum Mubin, has he forgotten his own origin? He challenges us, even as he forgets his own creation".

In other words, you're asking Allah SWT for an external proof, while you are a walking internal living proof. What proof do you need, when you are the proof itself? You dare ask Allah SWT for a challenge and your creation is itself the proof of the challenge. Then Allah SWT says, "The one who created you the first time, can recreate it again".

This is a logical argument that Allah Azza Wajal is bringing. And Allah SWT says in the Quran, "And he is the one who began the creation. And then he shall repeat it's all over again". And this is a very profound and interesting verse, that has caused some discussion amongst the Ulema on the phrase; "And it shall be easier for him to recreate".

Why is this verse potentially problematic to some theologians? The point that nothing is difficult for Allah SWT. For Allah SWT to say, "And I shall recreate, as I did it the first time. And the second time it'll be easier for me." (**as if** the first time was difficult)

Ibn Abbas RA responded to this very easily, and he said, "**If** there was a difficulty, **then** when you do it for a second time, it is easier. But **there was no difficulty** to begin with. And Allah SWT is simply making them understand that, '**If you think** there was any difficulty, surely to do it again is easier than to do it for the first time'".

So, Allah SWT is speaking to them at their level, that surely when somebody does anything for a second time, it is easier. So, in the realm of Allah SWT, nothing is difficult. He says "Kun Faya Kun". But if there were to have been an imaginary difficulty, surely recreation is easier than first time. And this is something we all know when we do something a second time it is easier.

So, this is the second genre. Under it are hundreds of verses where Allah SWT links belief in Judgment Day with the origins of man. And Allah SWT asks mankind to go back to his own creation and to understand how he was created. And that he shall be recreated same way.

The Heavens and The Earth

The third genre of versus also includes many dozens of versus under this one. In this reasoning Allah SWT tells mankind to examine the whole world around them. To observe the heavens and the earth. Just as the second reasoning was to examine yourself. The third reasoning is to examine the ecosystem.

And Allah SWT mentions in many of these verses that, "Don't you see that the one who created the heavens and the Earth is capable of creating or recreating something similar on to that?"

And Allah SWT says, "Don't they see the one who has created the heavens and the Earth, and he wasn't powerless in creating them. It wasn't difficult to create them. Don't they see, the one who created the heavens and the earth with such ease, is also capable of bringing the dead back to life?"

Once again, here we see an explicit linkage that, looks at the world around you. See the heavens and the earth; and realize that Allah SWT is capable of all things. So, this is the third genre, and that observing As-Samawat Al-Ard.

Bringing Dead Land Back to Life

The fourth genre is for specific natural elements within the Samawat Al-Ard. These are specific aspects of the creation around us, that Allah SWT in particular asks us to examine. And Allah SWT says, 'Look at this aspect. The one who is able to do that, is able to bring life back to the dead'.

Under this category there are many examples. The most common example in the Quran is that Allah SWT asks us to examine around us bringing of dead vegetation back to life, or dead land back to life. Now this is something that many do not fully understand growing up in America. Because in America we have a different type of soil, which generally speaking, is green even in the winter. Our soil is green in winter, even if it's not the same type of greenery. But it's a different type of soil.

When you go to a barren land, when you go to a desert land, you see different types of soils. And you have to see it to believe it. Where, throughout the year, land is completely baron and not a single leaf grows on it. Then a specific season comes, the rain season. And all of a sudden, that land that you could have sworn is never going to produce any fruit, it becomes greener than a dense Jungle.

And I've seen this with my own eyes when I was in Saudi Arabia. The change that happens three, it's unbelievable. There's a certain time where the amount of waterfall is perfect and that dead land is resurrected back to life. And this is something that the Arabs living in land, in that environment would have seen regularly. So, Allah SWT mentions that many times in the Quran.

For example, Allah SWT says, "Look at the effects of Allah's Mercy". Mercy here means rain. So, "Look at the effects of Allah's rain. How he brings the dead land back to life. This is the same way I shall bring the Mauta back to life. And indeed, Allah is capable of all things".

And this is at least a dozen or two dozen times in the Quran, that Allah SWT mentions the cycle of vegetation. And Allah SWT mentions that the leaves become yellow and then become they become green, and become alive again. Allah SWT says, 'You see this cycle around you. Not just the land, but you see it in the vegetation round you as well. Why can't you recognize that I can do the same for other species of life as well?"

Also, Allah SWT mentions the cycle of water. Also, Allah SWT mentions fire itself. So, Allah SWT says that, "This green tree, which is fed by blue water; it becomes this yellowish flame. Look at all of this cycle. The same way, surely I can also bring the dead back to life as well".

So, the cycles of other species, other life forms on this Earth, Allah SWT is saying that, "The one who can permutate those life forms, surely can permutate your life form as well". So, in this category and genre, Allah SWT asks us to look at specific aspects of the creation.

The Moral Argument

Now, category 5 is a very, very interesting one. Here Allah SWT uses, what modern philosophers have called the moral argument for the existence of God. This is something that was propagated very recently. I think only around 300 years ago. It is a very recent phenomenon of Western philosophy. But the Quran mentions it in this revelation.

Allah SWT mentions the moral argument for Judgment Day. What is the moral argument for Judgment Day? That this life is inherently unfair. And if there were no Judgement Day, then that would not be a perfection of Allah SWT's justice. This is an argument that Allah SWT uses in the Quran.

How can you deny the judgment day, when there's no justice in this dunya? And Allah SWT will not allow Injustice to go unpunished. So, the Quran uses the moral argument to prove the existence of Qiyamah. And Western philosophers only stumbled across this relatively recently. Allah SWT knows maybe from the Quran directly. And then they have a different category of how to prove the existence of Allah SWT.

There are a number of verses in this regard. Of them, Allah SWT says in the Quran, and this is a rhetorical question. A rhetorical question is a question whose answer is inherently within the question. And that answer doesn't need to be verbalized. A rhetorical question is meant to emphasize an obvious truth. It is not meant to actually question.

And Allah SWT uses a rhetorical question, because it is too self-evident to even respond.to It. So Allah SWT says, "Do you think we will make the Believers the same like the criminals? What is wrong with you? How are you judging?"

Here Allah SWT is slapping some sense into people. 'Do you think that a good person will be treated same as the bad person? That they'll live and they die and that's it. Nothing's going to happen to them. That's not fair'.

And in a more explicit verse, Allah SWT says in the Quran, "Do you think we are going to make the one who is good, and did good deeds, the same as the one who caused facade in the earth? And caused evil in the earth?" Meaning a person who is a mass murderer, a brutal dictator. That, "Do you think the one who suffered and the one who caused the suffering, that their lives will be the same? Will they be the same in their life and death? How evil is the Judgment that you make".

Meaning, how evil is it, that a mass murderer gets away with it. And even if he is killed, what's his one death compared to a million deaths that he caused. And what is one jail term in comparison to destroying an entire country, as so many brutal dictators have done.

So, Allah SWT is saying, what is wrong with you? How can you not affirm a judgment day when you see there are people who are being treated unjustly, unfairly? When you see people live their lives in piety. And they still from the worldly perspective, get the short end of the stick. They still might be harmed. Or they still die an unjust death. Or even if they die a normal death, they didn't get the reward of their good. Where is the good for that this pious person has done?

He lived his whole life in piety and yet he's struggling, living a difficult life. And another person, who is born into wealth, living the life of a pleasure seeker, not caring about the Akhira, and he lives an animalistic life and dies a normal death. Is that fair that this person gets to enjoy this dunya and he lives an evil life. And the righteous person was deprived of any good.

So, Allah SWT is telling us, "How evil is your ruling, to deny the Judgment Day. How can you make this decision? How can you critic that there's no judgment based upon the moral realities of the world that we live in?"

This is a very interesting argument to prove the day of judgment. And that is that, this world does not have Justice. There must be a place where there's infinite justice. And the one who does good or the one who does evil, shall taste the reward or the punishment for what they have done.

Purpose of Life

Argument number 6 that Allah SWT uses, is an argument that goes back to the divine wisdom of Allah SWT. That if there were no judgment day, and there were no heaven and hell; then life would become meaningless. Life would have no meaning.

And Allah SWT says in the Quran that, Qiyamah is linked to the purpose of creation of everything. Once again there's a direct cause of linkage. Allah SWT says, "Do you think we created you as a joke? As a jest? To waste our time? did you think that your whole existence wasn't for a higher reason? And that you are not going to return unto us?"

Notice how Allah SWT links belief in Judgment Day with his wisdom. If Allah SWT is all wise, there must be a judgment. It is as simple as that. If Allah SWT has Hikmah, and obviously he has Hikmah because of the creation around us.

The creation around us necessitate that Allah SWT is Aleem and Hakeem. That Allah SWT is perfectly wise. The one who is perfectly wise, does not do things foolishly. Does not waste time and energy in something useless.

Therefore, Allah SWT is saying, "We would not do something in vain". And again, there are a number of verses in this regard in the Quran.

Demonstration of Resurrection

The seventh genre of verses in Quran is of specific stories. Now, these are stories that we have to believe in. So, this goes back to point number one which was that we simply have to believe in Allah SWT in this regard. That a number of people challenged Allah SWT; or asked for proof; or to show them how resurrection occurs; and Allah SWT demonstrated. And then Allah SWT tells us in the Quran about their stories.

Now this is something that we simply have to believe in. But again, for those people who witnessed it, it was a miracle for them. For us, it is a miracle we believe in, although we didn't witness it. One of these stories in the Quran is the most obvious one. In Surah Baqarah it is mentioned that someone asked Allah SWT, "How can Allah SWT bring this entire city back to life, after it is completely destroyed?"

So, what did Allah SWT do? Allah SWT caused him to die. Meaning fall deep a sleep. Because sleep is the brother of death. And then Allah SWT caused him to wake up from that deep sleep after a very long time in a different era. The point of the story is that Allah SWT is demonstrating that he can resurrect the dead.

In another story in Surah Al Baqarah, Allah SWT tells story of a man who questioned resurrection, so Allah SWT caused him to die, and then the man was resurrected several years later. When he woke up, Allah SWT asked him how he was unconscious. The man though he was in comatose for a day. Then Allah SWT told him the truth.

Then the man sees his donkey, that had died and its bones were turned to dust as well. Then Allah SWT resurrected the donkey in front of him. This is another story where Allah SWT demonstrated that he has control over all things.

Also, in Surah Baqarah, Ibrahim AS himself asked Allah SWT that, "O Allah, show me how do you resurrect the dead". And Allah SWT says, "Don't you believe?" Ibrahim AS replied, "I believe O Allah. But I just want to make my Iman at ease and my heart at ease".

Our Prophet SAW said, and the Hadith is in Sahih Bukhari, "We have more right to have skepticism than Ibrahim AS". Skepticism here does not mean that we doubt in Allah SWT. Skepticism here means a wondrous skepticism. Not a doubtful skepticism. That how is Allah SWT doing it. And Not that Allah SWT cannot do it. There is a difference between the two.

Ibrahim AS had the first type of skepticism. Ibrahim AS said, 'I want to see how you are you doing it'. He said that, "I believe. I just want to see and it'll make my heart firm". So, Allah SWT told him to tear some birds in to pieces and then put the birds on the different places.

And then Allah SWT told Ibrahim AS, "Call them. They will come to racing back to you". So, this is another story of resurrection from the dead in the Quran.

A fourth story, is of Isa Ibn Maryam AS and the resurrection of a man called Lazarus in the Christian scriptures, in front of everybody's eyes. Another story is of Musa AS and the cow. Where he told Bani Israel to slaughter a cow and then the cow was brought back to life by Allah SWT. So, there are many stories in Quran and Sunnah of this nature, where people are resurrected from the actual death and other people see this.

So, this is something that, we believe in. But for those who saw it, it was an actual, physical demonstration of this reality. And the famous Mufassir of the Quran Sheikh Ash-Shanqeetee; he has a beautiful summary of all of these stores in Surah Al-Baqarah. Ash-Shanqeetee says that, "In these verses Allah SWT mentions three primary evidences of the resurrection of the Dead".

Number one, "The fact that he created mankind". As Allah SWT says, "Worship your Lord who created you and those before you. And that is because the creation of man and the creation of the mankind, is the greatest miracle and the greatest sign that he can create them all over again".

For example, Allah SWT says in Surah Al-Anbiya "As we created you the first time, we shall repeat it". And the verse in the Quran that says, "They ask, who will bring us back to life? say, the one who created the first time". And the verse in the Quran say, "say, the one who brought you the first time, will bring you back".

And another verse in the Quran that says, "Do you think that we were incapable of doing it the first time? Such that we cannot do it for the second time?"

Then he says that, the second evidence is the creation of the heavens and the earth. Which is mentioned in Quran, where Allah SWT says, "The one who made this Earth a platform and the heavens a Sky".

Then he mentions the third one, which is the life cycle of the water. And he says all of these are evidences that Allah SWT is reasoning with people that he will have a judgement day. So, these are the seven categories that were mentioned.

Benefits of Believing in Qiyamah

Now, what are some of the main benefits of believing in Qiyamah? What happens when we believe in the Qiyamah? There is simply no way to fully express the psychological and the spiritual and the Imani benefits of believing in Qiyamah. The impact on one's psyche, the impact on shaping one Paradigm of life, cannot be expressed in words. But we'll try to summarize a few points.

Firstly, beliefs in a Qiyamah provides a sense of morality and of self-discipline. It gives us a moral compass that is otherwise impossible to achieve. When we believe in Qiyamah, we act in an ethical manner. Honestly, avoiding sins, avoiding corruption, acting in a manner that is dignified, not taking advantage of an opportunity that we can commit a sin in; And of course, this is manifested in the level of Ihsan. We worship Allah SWT as if we can see him, even though we do not see him. But he sees us all.

When we believe in Qiyamah, it helps minimize our infractions, and our evil deed. In fact, it makes us live ethical Ives. It even impacts us in our private lives. And there is nothing to substitute that level of Muraqaba.

Muraqaba is Arabic means monitoring ourselves, knowing that there is a Qiyamah.

Number two, belief in Qiyamah motivates us to live. It motivates us to accomplish something. It motivates us to have a purpose in life, a meaning in life. When you don't believe in a Qiyamah, when you don't believe in God, life becomes really meaningless.

Because what's the purpose of living? What is the whole goal? And of course, one of the first philosophers to point out this contradiction, who himself was an atheist, was Nietzsche. The famous German philosopher who went mad at the end of his life. The famous philosopher who was one of the first to publicly Proclaim he was an atheist.

And atheism is a very modern phenomenon. In history of mankind, you will not find atheists up until two hundred years ago. And even two hundred years ago, it was just a handful of people. Only the last century, and especially the last half-century is when atheism has spread like wildfire. And Nietzsche was the first famous philosopher really to come out and Just out right deny God. As Nietzsche said in his infamous patches, Nauzubillah of the death of God, and 'we have killed God'.

In that passage when you read it, he mentions this parable of the group of people, that believe they have killed God; meaning the idea of God, and there's no God left. Nietzsche says that, "Do you not realize that in killing God, you have killed yourselves. When you extinguish the idea of God, you have extinguished your own existence. Life now becomes meaningless".

Then he writes in his philosophical way, "Now up Is down, and down is up. Dark is light, and light is dark". Meaning everything is gone, and there's nothing to anchor people to anything. In other words, morality is gone. Which we see happening right now. What was well known to be wrong yesterday is now embraced as being pure. Everything is up for grabs.

Once you remove God from the picture, not only morality, but your existence is destroyed. And therefore, we are witnessing the rise of a wave of mental disorders and depressions, the likes of which have never ever occurred in human history.

Just a few decades ago, growing up, teenagers did not undergo depression at the rate we're seeing now. Young men and women with their whole lives ahead of them. And now, if you look at it, every psychiatry journal is talking about it. It is because of the rise of meaninglessness in life.

Young men and women have to go to a psychiatrist, to a shrink, to a therapist, and take medication. Not that I'm saying it's wrong necessarily. But we have to ask ourselves the blunt question, why is there this influx of suicides? May Allah SWT protect all of us. But never in human history, have young men and women been committing suicide at the rate we see in this generation. And The way things are heading, it will get worse. Auzubillah.

But the question is why? Why are the rates of depression going up? To us it is self-evident. When you remove God and you remove religion and you remove an Akhira, life becomes meaningless and pointless. What's the point of living, when you just going to have to face one struggle, and one pain, and one rejection, after another?

What is the point when in the end, you are just going to be extinguished anyway; you might as well just extinguish yourself now, and save yourself the hassle of all that is going to happen. So, when you believe in a Qiyamah, believe it or not, it makes you alive inside. It makes your life worthwhile and meaningful.

The third point is linked to the second one. Not only does it make your life worthwhile, it gives you a sense of optimism. That the future will be better than the past. And this is explicit in the Quran that, "Whatever happens in this dunya, you have something to look forward to".

This is human nature, that if you're having a tough year at work. But you know that there's a raise coming in December. Or you're going to get a nice bonus in December. That reward gives you encouragement. Same way Allah SWT is saying, 'Don't worry about this world. Next world is better'.

Life can be very depressing let us be honest here. There's a lot of things that happen, that really affect us. But the future is brighter for the believer. And when the believer believes in Qiyamah, it gives a sense of peace that, 'The Akhira will be better for me'. So, it makes a person optimistic.

And this is what our Prophet SAW said, "Wondrous are the Affairs of the believer. For no matter what happens to the believer, the believer is a winner". How would the believer be a winner? Because he believes in an Akhira. If there was no Akhira, this life would truly be interpreted as a losing battle all the time.

Point number four, and this goes back to one of the ways that Allah SWT proves Qiyamah; That it gives a sense of justice and reckoning. All of us without exception have been harmed in this dunya. Injustice has occurred to us, whether it is of a small level. Where somebody says something nasty about you. The police pull you over for no reason, and gives you a ticket.

This is a minor thing. How about those whose families are being harmed by the tyrants? How about those who're being tortured in the Jails of the Zalimeen? How about those that have been incarcerated for no reason, except for speaking the truth. Those Ulema who are speaking truth to power. And they have been put into jail. Their families maybe even harmed or worse.

How about the dictators that have gotten away with killing a million people? How about the Uyghur brothers and sisters, whose organs are being harvested as of this very movement? And the government seems to be getting more and more powerful. And we can go on and on.

What hope do you give to those people, when there seems to be no hope? What is a sense of justice and anger, that legitimately will come, when you see your loved ones being harmed? Belief in Judgement Day won't take the anger away. But at least you won't go senseless. At least it will not cause you to go irrational. You will realize that the justice that you were devoid of, will be given to you on Judgement Day.

This is explicit in the Quran that says, "Just wait until Judgement day. We to are waiting". There are so many verses in the Quran, where the early Muslims who were being tortured, are explicitly told by Allah SWT, "Just be patient. You will see on Judgment Day what I do to them".

So, anyone who is suffering an injustice, even at a small level, or at a large level, Allah SWT tells them, "Be patient. You will see with your own eyes, what will happen on Judgement Day". Of course, this is mentioned many times in the Quran that, "They're going to be asked about what they have done".

Number five, of the benefits of believing in Judgment Day, is a sense of accountability, of checks and balances. In any Corporation, there's always checks and balance. If there isn't, the corporation goes haywire. Who is going to instill in us an accountability of our own deeds? Especially when, society wise when I get away with it. Especially when we have the opportunity to do something and we might not get caught.

Belief in Judgment Day makes us have checks and balances within ourselves. This is an explicit. Hadith in Musnad Imam Ahmed. It is a very interesting Hadith. So, in the days of Jahiliyyah, Arabs would brand animal so that it was not stolen and to tell that it's your own animal. But in the days before Islam, branding was done in a Harem manner.

They would brand by cutting off the ears and making a very unique pattern. It was a way of mutilating the animal. Auzubillah. The Prophet SAW forbade that mutilation. It was deemed Haram. And the Sahabi narrates, "I was cutting off the ear of my camel, and I heard someone behind me saying, 'O creation of Allah, know that the forearm of Allah SWT is going to be stronger than your forearm. And the blade of Allah SWT will be sharper than your blade".

He turned around to see who was it speaking, and it was the Prophet SAW. What is the Prophet SAW instilling in this man? That, "you're going to get away with it in this dunya. Nobody is going to punish you for mutilating your own animal. But Allah SWT's power will be stronger than your power. And Allah SWT's punishment is more effective than your punishment".

The Prophet SAW is linking that morality with that Hisab, in the man's heart. That you have to answer to Allah SWT on Judgement Day. And of course, we also know the Prophet SAW said in the famous Hadith that, "A person's feet will not move on Judgement Day, until he answers answer for 5 things. His money, where he got it from and what he spent it on. His time. His health. His wealth".

What happens when this Hadith is put in our minds? It terrifies us, as it should. We should think, 'where am I earning my money from?' What will I answer Allah SWT? What am I spending my money on? What am I doing with my time? With my youth? What did I do with that? All of these questions are Mahasabha.

Point number six, of the benefits of believing in a judgment day is that, it is a manifestation of Allah SWT's

Hikmah. Again, this goes back to the evidences as well. That we believe that Allah SWT is all-wise and when we believe in a judgment day, it affirms that Allah SWT is indeed all wise.

Point number seven, of the benefits of believing in Qiyamah, and this is explicit in the Quran as well, that it allows us to get rid of the feelings of jealousy for those who had more than us in this Dunya. If you look at our modern western culture, it is based on desiring what everybody else has. Trying to keep up with the Joneses, and the Lifestyles of the Rich and famous. Look at the magazine covers, look at the TV shows; it's all about the Creme de la Crème. and even they are all bankrupt.

People are taught that you should be like them. And Wallaahi, it's so difficult sometimes to not desire to be like everybody else. Why can't I have what they have? And Allah SWT explicitly says in the Quran, about the love for this dunya, and he asks us to not be concerned with it. And then he says that there is something better than this for us in the Akhira.

Allah SWT in multiple versus, tells us to not worry about this world. Allah SWT says, "don't worry about the beauty of this dunya. Whatever you have here, it will go away. What Allah SWT has will never go away". So, of the wisdoms of believing in Qiyamah is that this dunya becomes not that important to us. If we truly love the Akhira, then we're looking at a bigger goal than the dunya. If we don't have the Akira, this dunya becomes the ultimate goal.

And the final aspect is that, belief in the Akhira helps us in believing in other aspects of Ilm Al Ghaib. Because our Iman, much of it is something that we cannot feel. That we cannot touch. That we cannot see. And you have to believe in Al Ghaib to believe in Allah SWT. And when we believe in the Qiyamah, which is something that has an element of faith to it., we have to just take that leap of faith.

Allah SWT knows and we believe in Allah SWT. So, when we believe in Qiyamah, we are believing in the Ilm Al Ghaib. And when we believe in Ilm Al Ghaib, our Iman in Allah SWT is also made firm.

And Allah SWT mentions as well, of the wisdoms of the Akhira is to prove to the believers that Allah SWT's promise is true and to prove to the Kafir that they were wrong in denying Allah SWT's promise. Allah SWT says in the Quran, and this is one of the wisdoms of believing in Judgment Day that, "When the believers are resurrected, they're going to feel happiness that they were right".

So, when you believe in Qiyamah in this world, it will make you optimistic Insha'Allah, when you see it in the next world. And those who reject the Qiyamah in this world, it will be the beginning of the punishment when they see the Qiyamah, and they will feel a sense of despair.

Names of Qiyamah in Quran

Now, we will look at the names that the Allah SWT has used in the Quran for the Day of Judgement. So, we have around 25 names that we will mention in this book. This is a good attempt to delineate the proper nouns that Allah SWT use in the Quran to name the Day of Judgement.

Now, this is something that is well known that the Arabs and Quran in particular, when something is important, it has many names. So, the Quran has many names. The Prophet SAW has many names. Allah SWT has infinite names. So, the more important something is, the more names it has.

And Qiyamah, not surprisingly, is mentioned with hundreds of adjectives and at least two dozen actual proper names. So, we will go over every one of these names. And at least one or two places where they are found. And the meanings of these names.

Because if Allah SWT is using a name to describe the day of judgement, then we had better know what that name is. That name will tell us a description of the day of judgement. The name will tell us one of the main features of Qiyamah, that Allah SWT wants us to know about. Now, these names are not in any particular order, and they are definitely not in a chronological order.

Al Yaum Al-Akhir

So, we begin with the first name. The first name is Al Yaum Al-Akhir. And included in this is Akhira. Al Yaum Al-Akhir occurs 28 times in the Quran, as a proper noun for the final Judgment Day. And as for the term Akhira, it occurs more than 100 times. "Those who desire the Akhira". "Those who deny the Akhira". The Akhira is mentioned more than a hundred times.

Al Yaum Al-Akhir is mentioned in Surah Tawbah, verse 18, "The people who come to the Masjid are those who believe in Allah and believe in Al Yaum Al-Akhir". Because it will be the final day. After Judgement Day, there will be no sunset. After judgement day, there would be perpetual light in Jannah. There is no darkness in Jannah.

The literal final date of this existence shall be Al Yaum Al-Akhir. After Al Yaum Al-Akhir will begin a new world. It will begin a new realm, and a new dimension. That has nothing to do with this world. So literally, Judgment Day is the last day.

There will be no day after it. Because the next day that begins, will be Jannah or in Jahannam. And there will be nothing that will change over there. So, Al Yaum Al-Akhir is the final day. And the Akhira is the final life or the next life.

Yaum Al-A'zifa

Number two is Yaum Al-A'zifa. Yaum Al-A'zifa occurs only twice in the Quran. For example, it occurs in Surah An-Najm, verse 57. A'zifa means to come close. A'zifat Al-A'zifa means that which is very close, has come even closer.

So, the Qiyamah is called A'zifa because it is not that far away. Allah SWT says, "The people who reject Judgment Day, think it's going to come in a long time. They don't see it as something close by. We know it's very close by". And Allah SWT says in the Quran that, "The Judgment Day will come faster than the twinkling of the eye. Or even quicker than that".

And our Prophet SAW said, and the hadith is in Musnad Imam Ahmed that, "I was sent with the day of Judgment, at the same time. We were racing one another, that which one would come first. And I just beat the Judgment Day". And our Prophet SAW said, "Myself and Judgment Day have come like two fingers of your hand". The difference between our two fingers is very little. So, Judgment Day is right after the Prophet SAW.

The Prophet SAW said that, "Count 6 things before Judgement Day". Number one, "My death". So, the coming and death of the Prophet SAW is the first sign of Judgment Day. We have mentioned this in the first book of this series, the signs of the Judgement Day. So, Al-A'zifa is that which is close by, or that which is not far away.

Yaum Al-Ba'ats

The third name is Yaum Al-Ba'ats. Al-Ba'ats means the resurrection from the grave. And Allah SWT mentions Yaum Al-Ba'ats twice in the Quran. But the verb Yaba'atsu and its variations appear at least two dozen times. So, the verb has appeared more than the noun.

The example for the appearance of the noun is Surat Ar-Rum verse 56. Allah SWT says, "This is Yaum Al-Ba'ats. The day of the bodily resurrection. Every soul will be resurrected".

Yaum At- Taghabun

The fourth name is Yaum At- Taghabun. And Yaum At-Tagaabun occur in the Quran once. It occurs in Surah At-Taghabun number 9. It's actually a very interesting name. Our Scholars have spent many pages of tafseer trying to understand why is Qiyamah called Taghabun.

Because Taghabun has a very strange meaning. Ghabana means to cheat somebody in a business transaction. Al-Ghuban means deceit. Ghabana is to cheat someone. Typically, in a business transaction. That there was some type of subterfuge, or some type of covering up, or some type of great loss. Someone deceived someone.

Now, Taghabun means mutual deceiving. That two people are deceiving one another. Why is the day of judgement called Taghabun? There are multiple reasons given by scholars. First and foremost, one interpretation is that, there will be such unequal amount of reward and punishment. Where the people of Jannah are going to everlasting bliss. While the people of Jahannam are going to a life of sorrow.

There is no comparison. It is as if, there's a Taghabun going on for those who fail to purchase themselves on Judgement Day. Those who failed, failed miserably. And those who passed, passed with flying colors. So, this is one interpretation.

Another interpretation is that, groups of people are deceiving each other in this dunya. And on that day, their deceit will be manifest. Now, the primary meaning here is not business deceit. The primary meaning is religious deceit. The primary meaning is that groups of people are promising each other to not worry and to not believe in Islam.

That they will go to Jannah and they will be taken care of, if they reject Allah SWT. That if they believe in a false faith, everything will be fine. They're mutually deceiving one another. But they're helping one another in Batil and not helping one another in good. This is Yaum At- Taghabun. So, on Judgement Day, those people that were deceiving one another, will see the result of their deceit.

A third opinion, on why is Judgement Day called Yaum At- Taghabun is that, it is as if a person has cheated himself. It is as if a person has short changed himself even. In other words, you're supposed to sell yourself to Allah SWT. Meaning your deeds and purchase Jannah.

Allah SWT says in the Quran that, "Allah SWT's merchandise that he's selling is very expensive. His merchandise is Jannah". We need to purchase that Jannah. "The Believers have to purchase it from me". So, the motif is of selling our deeds.

Of course, Allah SWT doesn't need us to sell. It is Allah SWT being generous and the motif of selling your good deeds and getting Jannah in return. Now, what will be the one who sold this dunya for this dunya and didn't get this dunya or the Akhira? It is as if, he has deceived himself and cheated himself.

So, the third meaning of Taghabun is the man who does not get Jannah on Judgement Day. He has lived his life in the false illusion. He has deceived himself. And he shall come and see the result of his own deceiving on Judgement Day. So, therefore, Allah SWT calls Judgement Day Yaum At- Taghabun.

Yaum At-Talaq

The next noun of Judgment Day is Yaum At-Talaq. It occurs only once in the Quran, in Surah al-Ghafir verse 15. Allah SWT says, "So that they would be warned about the day of Talaq". What is the day of Talaq? It is the day of Mulaqat. Mulaqat means to meet one another. And Talaq is again two people or two entities meeting one another.

Why is Judgement Day called the day of meeting? Because on that day, the accuser will meet the accused. Accused will meet the accuser. There will be no barrier. In this dunya, the Zalim can run away. In this dunya, the Tyrant can hide in his palace. In this Dunya, the oppressor will have his army. And on Judgement Day, that lady that was killed, the child that was murdered, that innocent man that was harmed; he shall face the oppressor directly.

They will meet face-to-face. There will be no barrier. And you should be able to sue that person for your Haqq on Yaum At-Talaq This is the first meaning of Yaum At-Talaq. That is, you meeting the one whom you have a complaint against.

In this Dunya the oppressor is usually protected. In this Dunya those kings and tyrants and any evil people, powerful people. And no one will protect the oppressed. No one will protect you against the oppressor. But on Yaum At-Talaq they will have to face.

Another meaning of Talaq is that the Prophets AS will meet their Ummahs. This is explicitly mentioned in the Quran, that every Ummah will come with its Prophets AS. So, we will meet our Prophet SAW. This is Talaq. The first time the believers will see the Prophet SAW will be on Judgement Day. And our Prophet SAW will recognize the believers. How will he recognize them? From the A'sar of Wudu. May Allah SWT make us amongst them.

Another meaning of Talaq is that the person will finally meet up with all of his deeds which he ignored in this dunya. So again, this is a powerful name. The day that you will meet up with your deeds whether they are good and bad. There is no hiding on Judgement Day. No one can hide from anyone or anything. Either it is for good or for bad.

There are things we don't want to hide from. We don't want to hide from the Prophet SAW. We want to meet the Prophet SAW. There are things evil people want to hide from. They want to hide from those on whom they have done wrong. They will not be able to hide. Every one of us will want to hide from our sins but we will meet our sins. So, this is the fifth noun of the Judgment Day.

Yaum At-Tanad

The sixth noun of Judgment Day in the Quran is also mentioned one time only. It is Yaum At-Tanad. It occurs in Surah Ghafir verse 32. Allah SWT says, "The believer in the Palace of the Firon, the one who kept his Iman secret; that believer said, 'O my people, I am worried for you about Yaum At-Tanad'."

Now what is Tanad? It comes from a word which means to announce. So Yaum At-Tanad means the day of announcement. There are no secrets on judgement day. Except if Allah SWT wills and protects. And we want to be among those whom Allah SWT protects. There is no veil on judgement day, except for those whom Allah SWT chooses to give that veil to.

Otherwise there is no veil. And every person's sins will be apparent to others, except if Allah SWT chooses to conceal them. Allah SWT says, "The criminals will be recognized by their markings". Our Prophet SAW said, "Every criminal and every traitor will have a flag sticking out from his behind, going up". Every traitor that betrayed his promise, his trust, his people, will have this issue.

On Judgment Day, every criminal, every Tyrant, every Zalim will be marked and Stamped. So, this is Yaum At-Tanad. Announcements are going to be made and judgments will be passed out publicly. Everyone will know the fate of everybody else. The righteous will know their own fate and the opposite will also know their fate.

Also, Allah SWT will announce the righteous. Especially those who deserve a high place. On Judgement Day, there will be categories of people on whom Allah SWT will announce. And that is Yaum At-Tanad. When you go through school, sometimes the principal announces these are the people on the Dean's List. This is similar to what will happen on Yaum At-Tanad.

When for the righteous, Allah SWT will announce their verdicts. And the opposite as well. Those who deserve the worst, not only will they get the punishment; but the punishment will be announced. So that the punishment is increased.

Also, Allah SWT will announce the Maqam of our Prophet SAW, which is Al-Maqam Al-Mahmood. That is also Yaum At-Tanad. That Allah SWT will announce the status of our Nabi SAW. This is a general public announcement for all of mankind.

Yaum Al-Jamee

The seventh name of Judgement Day is Yaum Al-Jamee. It comes word Jumma. It is called Jumma because everybody comes together on that day. The Masjids are packed around the globe on Jumma. It means the gathering of people.

And it is obvious why Qiyamah is called Yaum Al-Jamee. The noun, it occurs twice in the Quran. As for the verb and variations of the verb, this occurs at least a dozen times.

So, Yaum Al-Jamee is used because never in all of existence have all the people been gathered together. Never in the entire creation, has all of the creation been gathered simultaneously. Therefore, how could it not be called the day of gathering; when every single man and woman, every single jinn, every single Muslim and Kafir, every single animal even, will be resurrected.

Can you imagine every single species that had a Ruh will be standing in one plain? How could it not be called Yaum Al-Jamee, the day of the gathering. There has never been and there shall never ever be after that, the likes of the gathering of Judgment Day. Never before and never after will all of the creation be gathered at one time, one location, one place.

Yaum Al-Khuruj

The eighth name of the day of judgement is Yaum Al-Khuruj. Yaum Al-Khuruj is also mentioned only once in the Quran. However, the verb is mentioned a half a dozen time. The noun Yaum Al-Khuruj comes in Surah Al-Kahf verse number 42 of the Quran. It means the day of exiting. Meaning from their graves. So, on Yaum Al-Khuruj all of mankind will literally come out of their graves.

Yaum Al-Hisab

The 9th name is Yaum Al-Hisab. Yaum Al-Hisab occurs around five times in the Quran. So, it's not uncommon. It is a semi-common name. It is mentioned in Surah Ibrahim verse 41, and in Surah Ghafir verse 27.

We all know what Hisab means. It is the day the accounts are settled and the balances are done. The day when all the losses and the gains will be tallied up. Just like at the end of the year every corporation has its Hisab, on Qiyamah every man and woman will have their Hisab.

So, everything will be checked and verified. Everything that you brought into your house, your wealth, your time, the blessings of Allah SWT gave you and what you produced with that. The balance sheets will be checked. And of course, Allah SWT would be the one who will do that Hisab.

Now question that a lot of people ask is why is Qiyamah call Yaum Al-Hisab when some people will enter Jannah without Hisab. As we mentioned that many of these names don't apply to every single person. But generically they apply to everyone. So, it is true that Qiyamah is called Yaum Al-Hisab, and it is also true that a very small group of people will enter Jannah without Hisab.

We want to be amongst them. But they will be a very small group of people. As our Prophet SAW said, they will be only 70,000 people, that will enter Jannah without Hisab. Out of billions and billions and billions of Muslims, the Prophet SAW said 70,000 will enter Jannah without Hisab.

So yes, it is true. But even in their case, technically they were supposed to get a Hisab, and they got out of it as a blessing from Allah SWT. So, still the default was there, that they're supposed to get the Hisab. Let's take an example we understand. That there is a straight A, super genius student. And by the time of the final exam, the professor says, 'Look you don't even need to take the exam. Go home, you will get the A".

This is. that level of rare occurrence that happens, that somebody is so well-grounded the professor will say, 'Don't worry. Just go home'. That he showed up for the exam. He was technically required to take the exam. But an exception can be made. So, just because the exception is made, we don't say there's no exam for the people. They're still going to be the exam. And there will be the Hisab.

Yaum Ad-Deen

The tenth name of Judgment Day is Yaum Ad-Deen. And of course, this one, we know it because this is in Surah Al-Fatiha. It is actually, in chronological order, of the Quran, the first name that is mentioned. And throughout the Quran Yaum Ad-Deen is mentioned around four or five times.

It is mentioned in Surah Al-Hijr verse number 35, where Allah SWT is saying to Shaitaan that, "You will have until Yaum Ad-Deen". Now, the word Deen in Arabic has a number of meanings. And its meaning in Yaum Ad-Deen is different than its meaning in phrase, 'Our Deen is Islam'.

The word Deen is a very deep word, that has multiple meanings. When we say, 'Our Deen is Islam', it means to submit based upon a methodology or law. So, to have a Deen means you have a methodology. And our methodology, our laws, our Paradigm is Islam. That's the meaning of Deen over there.

However, Deen also means to be judged. So, **Malik I Yaum Ad-Deen** means Master of Judgement Day. Because in this meaning, Yaum Ad-Deen is the day of judgement. It means the day when the verdicts will be passed. It means the day of recompense, the day when you will get what you deserve.

Al-Haqqah

The eleventh noun of Yaum Al-Qiyamah is Al-Haqqah. It occurs only three times in the Quran, in the first 3 verses of Surah Al-Haqqah. Al-Haqqah comes from the word Haqq. And Al-Haqqah is the Haqq that cannot be denied. The Haqq that is inevitable. That which is the most Haqq of everything that is Haqq; this is Al-Haqqah.

So, Allah SWT calls Qiyamah the truth of the truth, or the essence of the truth, or the truth that cannot be denied, or the inevitable truth. All of these is what Al-Haqqah means. So, it is the truth that no one can deny. We can also say that, it is the truth because, everybody will see their true selves. This is another meaning.

So, you have two connotations of Al-Haqqah; the day and then the people. As for the day, you cannot deny it. It is going to happen. Your verbal denial does not change that. Al-Haqqah also means that, people can have a false illusion. They can be Munafiq in this dunya. They can pretend to be righteous. And Al-Haqqah will expose the Haqq from the Batil.

Al-Haqqah will sniff through and you will know the true value of a person. You might have thought a person to be worthless and on Judgement Day he will be of the highest quality of people. You might have thought on another person to be righteous and on Judgment Day the opposite will be told. So, Al-Haqqah separates the truth and falsehood.

Yaum Al-Hasrah

Number twelve of the nouns of Judgment Day is Yaum Al-Hasrah. Yaum Al-Hasrah occurs only once in the Quran and that is in Surah Maryam verse 39 that says, "Warn them of the day of Hasrah". Hasrah in Arabic, is the worst level of regret and remorse.

But in Arabic, you have levels. Hasrah is the most powerful manifestation of regret. There is no word that is more powerful and how much you regret something then Hasrah. The Judgment Day is called Yaum Al-Hasrah for obvious reasons. Because it's one thing if you purchased the wrong car. But imagine you regret of wasting a life; and that's it. There is no more chance. The rest of eternity will be Jahannam.

What type of Hasrah will that person have? That is Yaum Al-Hasrah. The day of infinite remorse, of infinite regret. There will be no regrets that is worse than the day of Hasrah. And even though Yaum Al-Hasrah occurs only once, the concept Hasrah on Judgement Day occurs multiple times in the Quran.

For example, it occurs in multiple versus of Surah Az-Zumar. Allah SWT says that, "On Judgement Day the person will say, 'Wo on to me. How much regret do I have?'". Now, our Scholars also mention that Hasrah shall occur to everybody on Judgement Day. Even the righteous will have a level of Hasrah.

Because the righteous will blame themselves, even though they're getting into Jannah. Once you get into Jannah, there is no Hasrah. But until that time, our Scholars mentioned, even the rightious might feel a twinge of Hasrah for not doing even better, to get to a higher place in Jannah.

This would include the Shaheed as well, because we learn from the Quran and Sunnah that the Shaheed will say to Allah SWT, "Send me back to this dunya, so that I will come back 10 times. So that I get even more". Of course, the Hasrah of the Believers is not like the Hasrah of the Kafir. There's no question about this.

For sure, the believer obviously is getting it to Jannah, so Alhamdulillah. But there will be this twinge, 'Why didn't I do more? I could have done better. I'm getting into this level of Jannah. I could have gotten higher level. But I did not get that level'.

So, our Scholars say it is called Hasrah, because everybody, without exception, will have an element of regret. But obviously the Kafir will have the worst amount of Hasrah on judgment day.

Yaum Al-Khulud

Number thirteen of the names of Judgement Day is Yaum Al-Khulud. It is mentioned only once in the Quran is Surah Al-Kahf that. And interestingly enough it is only mentioned in the context of the Believers entering Jannah.

It is mentioned in a positive manner, that on Judgment Day, they will be entering Jannah, and Allah SWT says, "Indeed that is going to be the day of eternally blissful life". So, for the people of Jannah, Qiyamah is called Yaum Al-Khulud. Khulud here has a positive connotation. Khulud here is a blissful eternal life.

And Qiyamah is the beginning of that blissful eternal life. Because for the believers, especially for the righteous of the believers, Qiyamah will not be a pain. Qiyamah itself will be a blessing. Qiyamah itself will be an easy. So, for them the Qiyamah will itself begin the blessings, and it will then culminate in the opening up of the gates of Jannah and the Angels telling them to go inside.

Yaum Al-Qiyamah

The Fourteenth name of Judgement Day is the most common name in the Quran for the day of judgement. Without a doubt, it overshadows all other names. And it is Yaum Al-Qiyamah. Yaum Al-Qiyamah occurs a staggering seventy times in the Quran.

There is no other name that is even in the same ballpark figure as Yaum Al-Qiyamah. And Allah SWT mentions, "Mankind asks, 'When will this Yaum Al-Qiyamah occur?'" Now, Yaum Al-Qiyamah means the day of standing. Why is Judgement Day called the day of standing?

There are a number of reasons. Number one, because on that day Allah SWT will come. It is in the Quran. And the Angels will have lines behind them. And when Allah SWT appears, what will the mankind do? Every single creation will stand up in Majesty of Allah SWT. So, this is Qiyamah. Everybody will be standing.

Number two is that, on that day Allah SWT will bring out the witnesses who will testify against or for the people. And these witnesses will be standing in front of the people whom their testifying against. This is mentioned in Surah Ghafir verse 51, "On that day, the witnesses will stand up and testify".

In the courts of old, the people would be sitting down, except for the witness. So that everybody is paying attention to the witness as he is giving the testimony. In our time, the witnesses sit on a special chair in front of everyone and that chair is raised up.

But in those days, when you had a case, the judge will be sitting down and the witness would stand. So that it's understood that this is a very important movement and everybody's is paying attention and you must speak the truth. Same way on Day of Judgement the witnesses will stand up and they will testify for or against their people.

The third reason why it is called the Qiyamah is because, Allah SWT will cause all of the creation to stand up from their graves. When they get out of their graves, they will put their dust out and they will be standing up.

The fourth reason, why Qiyamah is called the Qiyamah is that, Allah SWT will place the scales of justice. And Justice will be standing over there.

And the fifth reason why it is called Qiyamah is because everyone will be standing in panic and anxiety. No one will sit down on Judgement Day because of the anxiety. When you're nervous, you cannot sit down. When you're nervous, your pacing, you're walking around. So, in Qiyamah everyone will be standing up, walking here and there.

Yaum Al-Fasli

The fifteenth name of Qiyamah in the Quran is Yaum Al-Fasli. Yaum Al-Fasli is mentioned six times in the Quran. Three of them are is Surah Al-Mursalat. And then three times in other Surahs. What does Yaum Al-Fasli mean? It means to separate.

Why is the Qiyamah called Yaum Al-Fasli? Because on that day, everyone will be separated according to how they deserve to be separated. The Shaheed will be with the Shaheed. The Prophets AS will be with the Prophets AS. The righteous will be with the righteous. The Zalim will be with the Zalim. Everyone will be with their group.

Whichever group they belong to, that is the group they will be judged with, and in accordance with. So Yaum Al-Fasli is the date of categorization. This is the primary meaning. Another meaning of Yaum Al-Fasli is to clarify and to make things clear. Obviously Qiyamah is called Yaum Al-Fasli because that is the day everything will be made clear. Nothing will be hidden.

As-Sa'aa

The sixteenth name of Judgment Day is As-Sa'aa. This is perhaps the second most common name of Qiyamah. It occurs almost 35 times in the Quran, that Allah SWT calls the Judgment Day by this name. And sometimes, Allah SWT talks about establishing the As-Sa'aa, and Making the As-Sa'aa come.

And Allah SWT says in Surah Taha verse 15 that, "The Sa'aa is indeed coming. But I have decided to hide its timing". And Allah SWT says in the Quran that, "The earthquakes of As-Sa'aa are very catastrophic". Of course, As-Sa'aa means time or the Hour. But do realize that when we say **Hour**, when the Quran came down, the Arabs did not have watches, where an hour means 60 minutes.

It's a unit of time. So As-Sa'aa does not mean the 60 minutes in our time frame. As-Sa'aa means just a portion of the day, or the portion of the night. Now why is the day of judgement called As-Sa'aa? Our Scholars have tried to give some interpretation about why it is called As-Sa'aa.

Some of them said that, Allah SWT has called Qiyamah As-Sa'aa, because just like we know that there are hours throughout the day, and hours of the night, so to there will be a Judgment Day within the lifespan of this existence. That's one interpretation.

Another interpretation is that it is called As-Sa'aa because, in the eyes of Allah SWT, even though it seems like an Infiniti to us, it will just go like an hour for him. And this is in the Quran as well that, "a day in the eyes of Allah is like a thousand of your years". That time is different in that dimension. Obviously, Allah AWT is above time and space. So, one interpretation is that As-Sa'aa means that, in the eyes of Allah SWT, it will be over very quickly.

Others have mentioned that, it is called As-Sa'aa because for the believers, it will go very quickly. In fact, one Hadith says, "The Momin will feel like the day of judgement is like the time between Asr and Maghrib". Meaning the believer will feel the Qiyamah is over very quickly.

Yaum Al-Wa'eed and Yaum Al-Ma'ud

For number 17 we can have two names in it. Both from the same root. The first of them is Yaum Al-Wa'eed. And the second of them is Yaum Al-Ma'ud. Both of them occur only once in the Quran. Yaum Al-Wa'eed is Surah Al-Kahf verse 20. Allah SWT says, "The trumpet will be blown that is Yaum Al-Wa'eed".

Now, the word Wa'eed in Arabic is different than Wa'ad. Arabic is such a precise language. When you promised someone with something that the person will anticipate, he wants it, he is looking forward to it, that is called Wa'ad. And when you promise someone with something that he's not looking forward to, that is called Wa'eed.

So Wa'ad is a positive promise and Wa'eed is a threatening promise. Wa'ad is a promise that, if you finish all of this in time, you'll get a raise. While, Wa'eed is the punishment from your mother and father if you misbehave. Allah SWT calls Judgement Day Wa'eed, because obviously it is the day that the threats will be enacted against those who rejected.

So, it is Yaum Al- Wa'eed for those who rejected and for those who are impious. That is the day all of these threats are going to catch up to them. And so, Allah SWT calls it Yaum Al- Wa'eed. Yaum Al-Ma'ud is of course only once in the Quran, in Surah Al-Buruj. Yaum

Al-Ma'ud means the day that has been promised. There's no negative or positive. It is a promise day. Allah SWT promised it and it is going to happen.

Of course, the concept of Qiyamah being a promise day is mentioned throughout the Quran. It is mentioned in Surah Yaseen that, "This is the promise that Allah SWT said is going to happen".

Al-Waqi'ah

Number eighteen occurs twice in the Quran. It is the word Al-Waqi'ah. Which occurs in the Surah Al-Waqi'ah and in Surah Al-Haqqah. Al-Waqi'ah comes from the root Waqa'a and Waqa'a means it has occurred.

Waqi'ah is the sure event that will occur. The event that is so true to occur, in might as well have occurred already. Al-Waqi'ah can also mean the occurrence that shall occur. The event that will eventualize.

As-Sa'kha

Number nineteen is As-Sa'kha. It occurs only once in the Quran, in Surah Abasa verse 33. As-Sa'kha is a loud noise. An extremely terrifying noise. A noise that shakes you to the core. So, Allah SWT calls Judgment Day As-Sa'kha, according to some scholars, because of the trumpet.

And some scholars say it is because of the chaos and the noise on Judgement Day. Which will be very loud, for those whom Allah SWT does not protect. once again all of the all of the terrifying adjectives, the believers will be protected from it. They will not have these terrifying adjectives. And the higher their Iman, the more they should be protected from the terror of Judgment day. But all of these adjectives apply primarily to those who rejected Islam.

Ta'mma-Tul Kubra

Number twenty is At-Ta'mma or Ta'mma-Tul Kubra. And it occurs in Surah An-Nazi'at verse number 34. Ta'mma is a tragedy. It is a calamity. Ta'mma-Tul Kubra is the biggest Calamity. Now, in Surah An-Nazi'at, if you read the context, it is about those who are going to Jahannam at the end of it.

And Allah SWT calls Judgment Day for them, '**your biggest tragedy**'. Of course, it is their biggest tragedy. The biggest catastrophe that has ever happened to the Kuffar is going to be Ta'mma-Tul Kubra. As they will be going to Jahannam.

Yaum Al-Aseer

Number twenty-one of the names of Judgement Day is Yaum Al-Aseer. It is mentioned twice in the Quran, in Surah Al-Furqan and in Surah Al-Muddaththir verse 9. Yaum Al-Aseer translates as the most difficult day.

In both of these circumstances, Allah SWT mentions that it is for the Kafir and not for the believer. So Yaum Al-Aseer is a description for the Kafir, not for the Momin. For the Kafir it is not going to be an easy day. It is going to be a difficult day.

Al-Ghashiyah

Number twenty-two is Al-Ghashiyah. Al-Ghashiyah only occurs once as a proper noun. Al-Ghashiyah comes from the verb Ghashah. And the means to envelope, or to cover up. So, Al-Ghashiyah is that switch is so terrifying that your thoughts will be so covered up with judgement day, you will have no energy to think about anything else. You will be overwhelmed.

May Allah SWT protect us. Any time a tragedy happens, what you think about is that tragedy. Everything else gets out of your mind. Everything is just expelled from your mind. Just one thing stays on your mind. It is human nature. So, Allah SWT calls the Judgment Day the one thing that when it happens, you will have no energy, or luxury, or time to think of anything else. It Shall overwhelm you, and over conquer you.

Other scholars mention as well that, Al-Ghashiyah means that it will envelope you in its occurrences. So, one can put it this way, Al-Ghashiyah can be internal with your thoughts, or external with what's going on. Both of them can apply. You're going to be so overwhelmed, that you will have no time to do anything else, externally and internally.

Al-Qari'ah

Number Twenty-three is Al-Qari'ah, and it occurs in Quran 3 times and that is in Surah Al-Qari'ah. The word Qari'ah has the connotation, generally speaking, of the sharp crack of a whip. It also implies the trembling that occurs because of a fear. So, Al-Qari'ah has the implication of something causing you to be terrified. That your hearts are trembling.

Another meaning of Qari'ah is to leave something barren. Because you will come to Allah SWT completely barren. You will not have the entourage you had in the dunya. You will not have the luxury. You will not have the false illusion that one might have in this world of power and fame.

Of course, the Hadith mentions this that, "People will be resurrected barefoot, naked and uncircumcised. As the day their mothers gave birth to them. They were going to come to Allah SWT with nothing other than their deeds".

Yaum Al-Mashood

Number twenty-four is Yaum Al-Mashood. It occurs only once in the Quran is Surah Hud verse 103. Yaum Al-Mashood means the witnessed day. Once again, never in all of the history of existence, will so many people witness one another. They will be bear witness and witness either against and for.

Never have all of the species, that is the Jinns and the Humans, and the Muslim and the Kafirs, and the men and the women, and the animals and the humans; have witnessed and watched one another before, the way they will on Judgement day. On top of this, the Angels will be looking. On top of this, Allah SWT himself will be there.

Yaum-un A'busun Kamtareer

Number twenty-five, some scholars have said that, of the names of Judgment Day is Yaum-un A'busun Kamtareer. Because it's in the Quran. A'busun means scowling. And Kamtareer is a gloomy face, or a face of dread. So, they are very similar in meaning. The point here is that those who get the results negatively, meaning a bad result, they will be scowling the worst scowl. They will be angry or sad.

Improper Nouns of Qiyamah

These are the twenty-five names that we have gathered together. Definitely the Quran mentions at least around two dozen proper nouns for Judgment Day. Around half of these only occur once. Like At- Taghabun, At-Talaq, At-Tanad, Al-Haqqah, Al-Hasrah, Al-Khulud, As-Sa'kha, At-Ta'mma, Al-Ghashiyah, Al-Wa'eed, Al-Ma'ud.

More than half of these names only occur once. And these names that are only occur once, interesting enough they're always in the Maki Surahs. And they're always in a very powerful manner, that is describing Judgment Day against those who rejected. So, Allah SWT uses these very specific nouns against those who reject.

There's a very explicit verse in the Quran in which Allah SWT says that, "On that day, the believers will be far away from all of that terror". So, all of the negative adjectives that are there, they will not apply to those who believe in Allah SWT and prepare for Judgment Day.

And this is something that is explicit in the Quran. Allah SWT says in the Quran that, "On that day faces will be laughing, shining bright". And Allah SWT says is in the Quran, "They're going to come back to their families. This is my judgment. I knew that I will meet my Hisab".

So, there are evidences that clearly showed that it is not going to apply to those who believe in Allah SWT.

Also, there are fourteen Surahs in the Quran named after Judgement Day. Of the names of the Surah named after Judgement day are Surah Ad-Dukhan, Surah Al-Waqi'ah, Surah Al-Hashr, Surah At-Taghabun, Surah Al-Haqqah, Surah Al-Qiyamah, Surah An-Naba, Surah At-Takwir, Surah Al-Infitar, Surah Al-Inshiqaq, Surah Al-Ghashiyah, Surah Az-Zalzalah, and Surah Al-Qari'ah.

So, these are the 14 surahs that are explicitly named after Qiyamah in the Quran. Even though sometimes the name is not a proper noun. For example, Az-Zalzalah is not a proper noun. It is an adjective. So, Allah SWT did not call Judgement Day Yaum Az-Zalzalah. But it is described that way.

So, there are at least two dozen names in the Quran that Allah SWT has given proper nouns to of Qiyamah. And there are at least three to four adjectives in the Quran of Qiyamah. Sometimes, Allah SWT mentions Yaum Al, and then a full phrase. This is not a name. It is a description.

For example, "On the day that no soul will benefit another soul". For example, "On that day, the one who has done Injustice, no excuse will be accepted". For example, "On that day money and children will be of no benefits". For example, "The day there is no doubt about it". For example, "There will be no bargaining on that day".

There are a few more examples. These are not proper nouns. These are descriptions of the day. You can say that Allah SWT has described the day with many adjectives, with many descriptions. But these are not proper nouns.

Events of the Judgement Day

Now, we will begin by discussing the actual Judgment Day. So, what's going to happen on Judgement Day? The scholars have mentioned up to 12 things that will happen. And some of these are mentioned with different nouns. So, we will discuss should they be taken as two separate things, or should they be the same things, that are being described differently.

We will also discuss the order of all of these 12 events. Because the order is not mentioned in the Quran or Sunnah. For example, there's going to be Mizan, and there's going to be Hawd, and there is going to be the Ard, and there's going to be the Hisab. Which order we will they come in? In these cases, we have to make an educated guess usually.

Because it makes sense that the Hawd is a place where the righteous are going to drink from it. That is going to take place, obviously after the resurrection. So, we will try to piece it together. But in the end of the day, there is no explicit evidence for the order of all of these things. Keep this point in mind.

So, what are the table of contents for judgement day? One of the great Scholars of theology, his name was Imam al-Safarini RA. He wrote a number of books about theology. And his books are very descriptive. Some of the most descriptive books of theology are his. Especially when it comes to the day of judgement. Imam al-Safarini RA mentions that there's going to be 8 things that will happen on the day of judgment. And he lists them.

We'll quickly go over them and then I'll add some more. Number one, Al-Ba'ats; which is the resurrection. Number two, An-Nushur; which is when you will come out of your grave and you're going to run helter-skelter. Number 3, Al-Hashr; which is the Gathering. Number four, Al-Qiyamah, or the Qiyamah, the standing up itself. Number five, Al-Ard, which is the showing of the deeds. Number six, the Judgment itself, whether on the right or the left hand. Number 7 is the Hisab. Number 8 is Al-Mizan or the setting up of the scales.

He didn't put it in order. He just mentioned eight things that are going to happen. Now in this list, he actually did not mention many things. Of them is the blowing of the trumpets, which will happen on Qiyamah. Of them, that he did not mention, something that is in the Quran; and that is the coming of Allah SWT. It is in the Quran that, "Allah SWT and the angels will come lined up in rows".

He also did not mention the seeing of Allah SWT. He did not mention the Shafa'a of Prophet SAW. He did not mention the Hawd. And the Hawd is translated as the Cistern or the pool of water. He did not mention the Sirat. He did not mention the Wurud. And he didn't mention the Qantara. Which according to one Hadith, is the final plane before the Gates of Heaven.

There is an open area before the gates of Jannah. To the back is Jahannam, and to the front is Jannah. And there will be a mini Hisab on the Qantara. And that Cantera is the end stage of the day of judgement. And if you pass the Qantara, you will enter Jannah. Once you pass that, there's no going back. But there will be some people who will be pushed back in Jahannam which is right behind and they will have to deal with certain things.

The Trumpet

So, the first thing that will happen on Judgement Day is the blowing of the trumpet. The blowing of the trumpet is mentioned exactly 10 times in a specific, direct, and explicit manner. And indirectly and implicitly, more than 10 times. And the explicit phrase is always with Nufikha Fis-Soor or Yanfuku Fis-Soor.

Of them, is Surah Taha verse 102. Allah SWT says, "On that day there will be Nufikha Fis-Soor". In Surah Yasin Ayah 51 and Surah Al An'am verse 73 as well. Surah Al An'am is the first time that this phrase is mentioned in the Quran. It is a very powerful verse.

Allah SWT says, "To him shall be the kingdom, to him shall be the power; the day that the trumpet will be blown. So, the one who controls that day, controls every day before and after. To him belongs the kingdom the day the trumpet shall be blown".

So, what is AS-Soor? There are two opinions. Imam At-Tabari RA mentions in his tafseer of Surah Al An'am verse 73. He says that, the first opinion is that, As-Soor is a trumpet. And we all know what a trumpet is. Now, in those days, trumpets would be typically made from the horns of animals. In our times, we create them from metal and other things. In those days, especially the

Jews used curled horns of the animals specially the Rams.

There is another opinion as well. And At-Tabari RA ascribes this to Ibn Abbas RA. And this opinion is that As-Soor is the plural of Sura. Which means image of a man. So, the Ayah translates in to, "The day that the souls will be re breathed In to the bodies of men and women.

However, the second opinion has essentially been discarded after that era. And no major scholar has ever held this opinion. And that is because, both the Quran and Sunnah seem to be very explicit that the Soor is an actual trumpet, and not the images of men or the shapes of men. Although, linguistically it makes sense.

Nonetheless, basically all Ulema agree with this interpretation that As-Soor is an actual trumpet. And there are multiple evidences. Of them are explicit hadiths. The most famous amongst them is in Sunnah Tirmidhi, Hadith number 3244. Abdullah Ibn Amr Al-A's said that, "Once a Bedouin came to the Prophet SAW and he said, "Oh Messenger of Allah SAW, what is the Soor?' He said, 'It is a Horn that you blow into'".

So, it is an actual horn that will be blown into. That's quite explicit. This is actually very simple. But there's also evidence it's in the Quran itself. And of them, some of our scholars have pointed out that, Allah says in the

Quran that, "Then it shall be blown into it again". Now, the souls will not enter the bodies on Judgement Day twice. But an actual trumpet can be blown in to twice.

Now, the blowing of the trumpets is mentioned 10 times in the Quran explicitly, and over a dozen a Hadith mention the concept of it as well, very explicitly. Of them is the famous Hadith in both Bukhari and Muslim. Which is the highest level of authenticity.

In this Hadith Abu Huraira RA narrates that, one day, a Jewish person was selling a piece of merchandise. And a Muslim man purchased it from him. But the Muslim man gave him a smaller price. They were trying to negotiate. So, the Jewish man said, "No way I'm going to sell this to you for this price. And I swear by the one who shows and preferred Musa AS over all of mankind".

He is Jewish, so he's making a Kasam of Musa AS. As Musa AS is the Prophet for Jews. So, when he said this, one of the Ansar stood up and slapped him across the face. And the Ansar said, "How dare you say the one who chose Musa over Mankind and the Prophet SAW is alive amongst US". And this the shows that sometimes this over sensitiveness, which is very common in our culture, for some reason, can be problematic. Where the smallest thing is read into.

Now this person did not clearly intend any disrespect. He's a Jewish person. What do you expect him to say?

Who is he going to take a Kasam on? He's merely praising his Prophet, in a matter that he believes in right. Subhan Allah, where did this Jewish person go to complain? He went to the Prophet SAW.

Imagine this Hadith here. He said to the Prophet SAW, "Ya Abl-Qasim'. Because the Jews would address Prophet SAW with his Kunya. So, he said, "I am a person who has protection and honor from you". In other words, I'm a citizen of Medina. "How can I be slapped by one of the people here".

Notice he is complaining directly to the Prophet SAW. So, the Prophet SAW said, "Why did he slap your face?" So, the Ansari was called and he explained, and the Prophet SAW became angry. Such that the redness was clearly apparent on his face.

And he said, "Do not have this argument, who is better than each other between the Anbiya of Allah SWT. Do not go down this route. Because, when the trumpet will be blown and all who are in the heavens and earth will fall down unconscious, and then it will be blowing again; and I will be the first to raise my head and I'll be the first to come out to the grave and I will see Musa already holding on to one of the pillars of the Throne of Allah SWT. So, I do not know, was the first time that She fainted, enough that he doesn't have to faint again? Or did I actually resurrect before him? Or was he resurrected before me?"

Now, the point of the point of this Hadith is very deep. So, remember Musa AS fainted in this world when he asked to see Allah SWT. Quran mentions that when the trumpet is blown, all who are in the heavens and earth will fall unconscious in a faint. And same word is used for fainting in Quran for trumpet being blown and Musa AS asking to see Allah SWT.

In other words, Prophet SAW is telling the Muslim that, "You do not know who is better". He is saying this to make both of them realize, especially the Muslim; and the Prophet SAW is so angry at the Muslim, for his overzealousness, that's his face is bright red. We should note that the prophet SAW would only get that angry very rarely. So that's the Hadith from which we learned there is something called the Trumpet being blown.

In Sahih Muslim we learn that the Prophet SAW said that, "The trumpet will be blown and everyone who hears the trumpets they will turn their head to the direction of the sound. Their heads will go towards that sound in an attempt to listen to the trumpet. The first person to hear it will be a man who is busy preparing water to feed his camel and he will fall dead on top of that water. Then all the people will fall dead". This is a graphic and vivid detail about the Trumpet.

In another Hadith in Musnad Imam Ahmed, our Prophet SAW says that, "The day of judgment will occur when two men will spread a garment in front of them. One is the buyer and other is the seller. But the trumpet will be blown before the trade is completed. Before the Garment is picked up. The hour will not be established until a man has milked the she-camel, and taken away the milk. But he will not be able to drink it. The hour will be established when a man is preparing water for his animal, but the animal will not drink from it. The hour will be established when a person has raised food to his mouth and he will not be able to eat it".

This is referenced in the Quran as well that, "The day of judgment is like the twinkling of an eye". Meaning it is going to come suddenly. There is no warning for the trumpet to come. This is explicit in the Quran and the Sunnah for the first trumpet that will be blown. All of these evidences clearly demonstrate the blowing of an actual trumpet, from which sound is going to be heard. Also, Allah SWT mentioned in the Quran "a loud noise" to explain the sound of the Trumpet.

Angel Responsible for Blowing the Trumpet

Now we know the name of the Angel is Israfil AS. Now Allah SWT does not mention Israfil AS in the Quran by name. But we know from the authentic Hadith, that the angel that the trumpet has been assigned to one special Angel.

This is very clear the Hadith. in Tirmidhi, where Abu Saeed Al-Khudri RA said, "One day the Prophet SAW came in a disturb State. he was perturbed". And the Prophet SAW said, "How can I relax and how can I be calm, when the one who has been assigned the trumpet, the one who is the companion of the Trumpet, has put it to his lips and his ears are paying attention and his forehead is looking in the direction, waiting for the command to come."

In other words, as some Ulama have derived is that the trumpet was raised to the lips. Of Israfil AS at that time and that's what disturbed the Prophet SAW. That the he SAW is telling the Sahaba that the time is very close. Because the Companion has been assigned the trumpet from the beginning of time. The Sahaba said, "O Messenger of Allah SAW, what should we do?" He SAW said, "Say, Hasbunallahu wa Ni'mal Wakil".

In another Hadith reported by Musnad Imam Ahmed, mentions that the Prophet SAW said that, "The companion of the trumpet, to his right is Jibreel AS and to his left is Mikael AS". But the name of the Angel is not mentioned. He is referenced as the companion of the trumpet.

Now the name Israfil being associated with the trumpet is something that is not found in the Quran or in any of the authentic Hadiths. It is found in tertiary sources and some uncertain Hadiths. However, there is unanimous consensus amongst the scholars that the name of the companion of the trumpet is Israfil AS.

The name Israfil, it is mentioned in one authentic Hadith, but in that Hadith the trumpet is not mentioned. Abd al-Rahman ibn Awf RA asked Aisha RA, the Hadith is in Sahih Muslim, "How did the Prophet SAW begin salah of Tahajud?" She said, "When he SAW would stand up for the prayer, he would say 'O Allah SWT, the creator of Jibreel AS, Mikael AS and Israfil AS, and the heavens and the earth, knower of the seen and unseen, guide me to the straight path".

Scholars have derived that the reason these three angels are mentioned in this Hadith is because Jibreel AS is the one who brings the Wahy, which is the nourishment of the Soul. Mikael AS is the one who is in charge of rain and food, which is nourishment of the body. And Israfil AS is in charge of the trumpet which will once again bring the body back to Life.

Ibn Hajar RA said that "It is something that is very commonly known that the companion of the Trumpet is Israfil AS". Imam Al Qurtubi RA say that, "All of the Nations, not just Muslims, have agreed that the one who will blow the trumpet is Israfil AS". So, it's not just belief of the Muslims. It is belief of the Christians and Jews as well. Now Israfil AS is called Raphael in Jewish and Christian tradition.

For example, in the Babylonian Talmud, the Three Angels that come to Ibrahim AS are Gabriel, Michael and Raphael. In the New Testament, in 1st Thessalonians, chapter number 6, it says, "The Lord himself shall descend from heaven, with the voice of the Archangel and with the trumpet of God. Behold in the twinkling of an eye, the last trumpet will sound and the dead will be raised".

This is very explicit even in the New Testament as well. The twinkling of the eye, the same phrases as Quran. Obviously, there are nuggets in the old and the new Testament that originated from Allah SWT, and are still there. We know it because they match up with the Quran. All of this is to say that the blowing of the trumpet and its association with Israfil AS are some things that are common to all three Abrahamic religions.

How Many Times will the Trumpet be Blown?

All scholars agree that the trumpet will be blown more than once because it's in the Quran. Surah Az-Zumar verse68 is the most explicit. Allah SWT says, "The trumpet will be blown. All who are in the heavens and the earth will fall down unconscious. Except those whom Allah has willed, will not fall unconscious". Then Allah SWT says, "Then it shall be blown again. They will all be standing up looking".

So, it's very clear that trumpet is going to be blown more than once. How many times more than once is where you find two opinions. The first opinion is that the trumpet will be blown three times. The second opinion is that it will be blown two times.

Many of our classical Ulema say that the trumpet will be blown three times. Of them are Ibn Al-Arabi RA, Ibn Taymiyyah RA, Ibn Kathir RA, Al Alusi RA, and Al-Shawkani RA. The majority of the Ulema have said that the trumpet will be blown three times.

The Quranic evidence that they present is that there are three adjectives that are used in the Quran for the blowing of the trumpet. Therefore, they have derived that each of these adjectives indicates a different blowing of the trumpet. The first adjective means "The blowing that shall frighten", and this is mentioned in Surah Al Naml verse 87. Allah SWR says, "On the day the trumpet will be blown, everyone in the heavens and earth will be alarmed, shocked, frightened".

The second is "The blowing of falling unconscious or dead". This is mentioned in Surah Az-Zumar verse 68. Allah SWT says, "The trumpet will be blown. All who are in the heavens and the earth will fall down unconscious. Except those whom Allah has willed, will not fall unconscious". The third one is also mentioned in Surah Az-Zumar which means the Blowing that will bring everyone back to life.

Therefore, the scholars drive from this that the first trumpet will terrify all of mankind. Shortly after this, there will be another trumpet that will kill all of mankind. Then there will be the third trumpet that will resurrect all of mankind.

The primary evidence for the trumpet being blown three times, is a very explicit Hadith, which is considered un-authentic by other scholars. It's a very long hadith that describes in vivid detail, Judgment Day from beginning to end. Ibn Kathir RA in his book "The Beginning and the End" mentions this whole hadith in its entirety. Then he says that this hadith is a well-known un-authentic hadith. Just like, "Seek knowledge even if you have to go to China". This is a well know

Hadith that is not authentic. Our Prophet SAW never said it.

This hadith says that, "There shall be blowing of the trumpets. The first trumpet will terrify all of mankind. The second will kill all of mankind. Then third will resurrect all of mankind". Based upon this, the Ulema extracted that there are 3 blowing of the trumpets.

The other position is that the trumpet will be blown only two times. The people will hear the first trumpet being blown. They will be terrified and then they will die. According to this group of Ulema the effects of the first and second trumpet being blown, as believed by the other group of Ulema, is put together in one.

When people will first hear the trumpet, they will be terrified and by the time it's finished, they will be dead. Then the second trumpet will resurrect everyone. This is the position of Imam Al-Qurtubi RA, and before him Al-Qushayri RA and after him Ibn Hajar RA, and also appears to the position of Ibn Abbas RA, Abu Qatada RA, and Hasan Al Basri RA.

It is evidently the stronger position for many reasons. Of them is that there's nothing explicit in Quran and Sunnah to prove the first opinion. But there is plenty evidence in Quran and Sunnah that indicates exactly two times the Trumpet being blown.

Of them, the first evidence which is the most explicit. Surah Az-Zumar verse 68 in the Quran. Because Allah SWT says, "Then it shall be blown again". And you only say again for the second time. Then there is no mention of the Trumpet being blown after this in the Ayah.

The second evidence is Surah Yasin which also mentions, indirectly, the trumpet being blown twice. "They are only waiting for one loud shout while they're still arguing over it. Then the trumpet will be blown and they're going to be coming out of their graves". So, Allah SWT is saying, the first one is a loud sound of trumpet that people will hear. This is about the death. Then the second one is about the resurrection.

The third evidence is in Surah An-Nazi'at. Allah SWT says that, "The day that loud terrifying noises is going to be done, it should be followed by the second blast". Ibn Abbas RA said that, "The first trumpet being blown shall follow the second time the trumpet is blown". Hassan Al Basri RA said that, "There are 2 trumpets to be blown. The first one of them, Allah SWT will cause the living to die, and the second one, Allah SWT will cause the dead to become alive gain". Then he quoted this verse.

The fourth evidence is a Hadith of the Prophet SAW. It is in Bukhari and Muslim. The Prophet SAW said that, "Between the two blowing of the trumpet is forty". Abu Huraira was asked, 'What is this forty, between the two blowing of trumpets? Is it forty years or forty days?" He

RA said, "I cannot answer. I don't know. I cannot say anything, that I didn't hear the prophet SAW say".

So, we don't know what 40 stages of time or time frames there will be between the first and second blowing of the trumpet. But the hadith very explicitly mentions two times trumpets being blown.

The Fifth evidence is a Hadith in Sahih Muslim that, "The trumpet will be blown. Everyone will look at it. They will fall down unconscious and die. Then Allah SWT will send the rain and the body shall be resurrected. Then the trumpet will be blown again and they will stand up".

The final evidence is in Abu Dawood, that our Prophet SAW said, "Jumma is the best day of the week and on the day of Jumma the first blowing of the trumpet, and on the day of Jumma shall be the second blowing of the trumpet". So Qiyamah will come on Friday and the resurrection will also be on Friday.

Saved from Trumpet

The final point to mentioned is that Allah SWT says that, "There will be a group of people who will save from falling unconscious".

One opinion is that Jibreel As, Mikael AS, Israfil AS and Malik Al Maut will be safe. Then Allah SWT will Ask Malik Al Maut to take soul of Israfil AS, then Mikael AS and then Jibreel AS. Lastly Allah SWT will take soul of Malik Al Maut. This opinion is also driven from the Hadith in Tabarani that mentions the trumpet being blown 3 times.

Now, we can't say anything about Musa AS, as the Prophet SAW himself said that he doesn't know if Musa AS is amongst those who are safe from the Trumpet. So, we for sure can't comment on it.

Ulema have various opinions on this. Ibn Hazm RA says that it will be most of the Angels. Ibn Suleman RA says, it will be Jibreel AS, Mikael AS, Israfil AS and Malik Al Maut. Ahmed Ibn Hanbal RA that, "This is the creation of Allah SWT in Jannah. They will not die when the trumpet is blown".

But at the end of the day, when the Prophet SAW is saying "I don't know". I think we should also say "I don't know". There will be some creation who will not fall unconscious and dead. Who they are? Allah knows best. We do not know.

And honestly, it won't affect us. Because we know that definitely we are of those who will hear the Trumpet being blown. But the trumpet, the first one, will not be heard by any Muslim. As no muslim will be on earth to hear the first trumpet. The first trumpet will be blown on a group of people who don't believe in Allah SWT.

Fate of Angels When Trumpet is Blown?

The next point is whether the angels will die when the trumpet is blown or between the Trump being blown. Now the popular opinion amongst most of the Muslim masses and even most of our scholars who wrote about this issue is that the angels will in fact die.

In fact, one of our scholars by the name of Al Munavi RA, he wrote a commentary of Imam al-Suyuti RA's book called Jami Al-Saghir. It is one of the largest books of hadith. Now in that commentary he wrote that there is unanimous consensus that the angels will die along with all of the creation.

The first and foremost of the evidences pointed out by the Ulema is that number one, the generality of the Quranic verses that everything and everyone will die and perish. There are a number of evidences from the Quran that everything will perish.

Allah Subhana WA Ta'ala says in Surah Al-Qasas verse 88 that, "Everything shall be destroyed except for Allah subhanahu Wa'ta'ala". From these general versus a number of our early scholars derive that yes even the Angels will perish. Of them is Qatada ibn al-Nu'man RA, the student of Ibn Abbas RA. Including Muqatil ibn Sulayman RA, who is one of the earliest Mufassir ever.

He died 150 Hira. He wrote a Tafsir that is the earliest printed tafseer that we have of the Quran. And a number of other Mufassir have the same opinion.

There is another evidence as well. This is an evidence that is found in a very long hadith in the Mustadrak al Hakim. But it is extremely weak. This Hadith states that the Malaika will die.

There is a third evidence that the Angels will die as well. This is the evidence that goes back to the hadith that is mentioned in the previous two chapters. Ibn Kathir RA said that this Hadith is well known even though it is of a weak chain.

In this Hadith Abu Huraira RA said that the Prophet SAW told them that, "Allah Subhana WA Ta'ala after he finished creating the heavens and earth, he created the trumpet, and he handed the trumpet to Israfil AS. Since then, Israfil AS has forever remained staring at the throne of Allah SWT, waiting until Allah SWT will command him".

Abu Huraira RA said, "O Messenger of Allah SWT, what is the trumpet?" The prophet SAW said, "It is a horn that is blown into". Abu Hurairah RA said, "how is it?" The Prophet SAW said, "It is huge and massive. I swear by the one who controls my soul that one circle of the trumpet or one circuit of this horn, is as vast as between the heavens and the earth. Israfil AS will blow this horn three times. First will terrify everyone. Second will kill everyone. Third will resurrect everyone".

Then the Abu Huraira asked Prophet SAW about the dead people. The Prophet SAW said, "The ones who are dead will not hear the first trumpet and they will be in their graves at peace. When Israfil will blow the trumpet for the second time, this will be when all who are in the heavens and earth will fall down dead. Except whom Allah SWT pleases".

Then the Malak al Maut will come to Allah SWT and he will say, "Oh Allah SWT all the people of the heavens and earth have died, except whom you have allowed to live". Allah SWT will say, "Who is left?" The Malak al Maut will say, "You are left. Because you are the high who does not die. The carriers of the throne are left. Jibreel AS is left, Mikael AS is left, Israfil AS, and I am left".

Allah SWT will say, "O Jibreel, Mikael and Israfil die". So, the Arsh will say, "o Allah SWT you will cause them die?" Allah SWT will say, "Be quiet for I have written that all who are under the throne shall die". So Jibreel AS, Mikael AS and Israfil AS will die.

Then Malak al Maut will come and he will say, "o Allah SWT I have taken their souls". And Allah SWT will say, "who is left?" He will say, "You are left o Allah, the carriers of your throne, and I am left". Then carriers of throne will die. No one will be left except Allah SWT and Malik Al Maut.

Then Allah Azza WA JAL will say to the Malik Al Maut, "You are a creation that I have created. I am Telling You to die". So, Malik Al Maut will die. Then no one will be left except Allah SWT. Then Allah SWT will say with his voice and a loud voice, "Is there any one left?" Then finding no one to respond, Allah Azza Wajal will answer himself, "I am the only one left".

These are the three evidences that tell us that the angels will die. Number one, the generalities from the Quran. Number two, a very weak hadith. Number three a very weak hadith. Is there any authentic evidence therefore that the Angels will die? clearly not.

There has been an alternative opinion. Of them is At Tabari RA, who mentions in more than one place that the Angels will not die. Of them is the famous Andalusian scholar. One of the most ingenious and eccentric minds to ever come from Andalus, Ibn Hazm RA. He wrote in his famous book Al Fisal, which is a five volumes book about all of the groups of Islam ever, from the time of the Prophet SAW, up until his time. It has four hundred years of Islamic history and theology all the different Fiqh.

He mentions about the death of the Angels in this book and he says, "There is no explicit evidence, nor is there ijma that the angels will die. If there was an evidence, I would have said this. There is no indication that causes us to believe that they will die. Because Jannah is a place where there is no death. The angels will be in Jannah and they were created in Jannah, and they shall live in Jannah".

He has the same argument about the other residents of heaven. And he makes the argument that death is the separation of the body from the soul. But the Angels don't have a physical body and a soul. So, their death cannot happen. Prophet SAW explicitly said that the Angels have been created from light. So, the Angels are not body and soul.

Also, there is a very interesting point by an early scholar of tafseer Al Wahidi RA, who died in the fourth century of the Hijra. He wrote a book on tafseer. Even though he did an explicit talk about the Trumpet and the Angels in his tafseer, he does mention that the Angels will live forever.

He derives this from a verse in the Quran. He says that, "When Iblees came to Adam AS and tempted Adam AS to eat from the tree, what did Iblees say to Adam AS?" And he quotes the Ayah of the Quran that says, "The reason why Allah SWT told you to not eat of this tree is that, if you eat from this tree you will become an Angel. You will become those who live forever".

Al Wahidi RA then says "Iblees said this because Angels live forever and do not die". So, this is his derivation that Adam AS knew that Angels don't die. If the Angels died, then what would be the temptation to eat from the tree?

Some ulema have also said that the angels do not die, based upon the hadith in Bukhari and Muslim. Which states that the Prophet SAW would make dua to Allah subhanahu wa'ta'ala "I seek refuge in you and in your glory, Allah. You are the one who is one and Only. You are the one who does not die. The Jinn and the Humans die".

Now, the evidence from this hadith is that the Prophet SAW did not mention Malaika. This type of extraction is based upon the opposite implication of the fact that the Angels are not mentioned.

Now, in the end of the day, there no explicit evidence whether the Angels will die or not. The fact of the matter is that there is no tangible benefit in knowing whether the Angels will die or not. But you should know that there is no authentic evidence that the Angels will die. The Angels are the inhabitants of Jannah. The trumpet has nothing to do with them. They're in a different world. The trumpet has to do with our world.

Also, in Surah Ghafir verses 15 to 17, Allah SWT says in the Quran that, "Allah SWT is the one who raises the ranks. The one who owns the throne. The one who sends Jibreel to whomever he wants of his creation, to warn them of the day of judgment. The day they will meet. On that day they will be in front of everyone. Nothing will be hidden in front of Allah SWT and them. To whom does the kingdom belong today? To Allah. Today everyone will get what they have earned and deserved".

Now, this is after the trumpet is blown. Not between the two trumpets. The Quran does not indicate that Allah SWT will say, "To whom does the kingdom belong today?" Then there will be dead silence. Then Allah SWT will answer himself.

Ibn al Jawzi RA was a great scholar. He wrote books on hadith and books on tafseer and books on Fiqh and books on Aqidah. He has a 9 volume Tafseer called Zad al-Masir. He says in his tafseer that, the phrase "To whom does the kingdom belong today?" will be uttered after this world. All ulema agree to that, but they have differed when it will be said.

There are two opinions. The first of them is that this will be said between the two trumpets, when no one will be able to respond. So, Allah will respond to himself. To "Whom does the kingdom belong today? To Allah". The second opinion is that this will happen on the day of judgement. Meaning after the second trumpet on the day of judgement. Meaning after the resurrection.

Ibn Abbas RA said, and note that this is not a Hadith, "Once all who are in the heavens and earth are destroyed and only Allah is left, Allah will say, 'Whom does the kingdom belong today?'; and no one will be there to respond. So, Allah will respond upon himself, 'To Allah'." Therefore, according to Ibn Abbas RA, this is between the two trumpets.

However, a number of other authorities including Ibn Masud RA have said that this is going to happen after the second trumpet, on the day of judgment. Ibn Masud RA said that, "Allah Subhana WA Ta'ala will gather all of the creation on the day of judgment, and the very first announcement to be made will be an Angel who says, 'To whom does the kingdom belong today?' Then all of the creation will respond and will testify to Allah SWT". He totally reverses the narrative as the entire creation responds to Allah Subhanahu wa'ta'ala.

Al Hashr

Now, the Hashr will take place right after the trumpet. So, at the end trumpet, when it is done, after that Hashr will take place. Al Hashr is the Arabic word that means to intentionally gather people or entities, who have been separated, for a higher purpose.

The word Hashr implies three things. Number one, that the gathering is done by a third party. It's done intentionally. It doesn't just happen randomly. Number two, that the people that are gathered, were not there in the beginning. They are gathered after. Number three, they're not gathered for no reason. They're gathered for a goal, for a purpose.

For example, in Surah Naml, Suleman AS calls all of his army and entourage of animals and jinn and beasts and soldiers to a war parade. The word used for the parade is Hashr. As he's the one calling them together and there is a purpose.

Also, in the story of Firon, when Allah SWT mentions that Firon wanted to have his magicians go against Musa AS' miracles, the advisors of Firon said, "Why don't we do it on the day of our celebration?" In Quran that day of celebration is worded as Hashr as well. As everyone will be gathered by the Firon. There's going to be the purpose of celebration.

Same way Allah SWT calls the first act of the Day of Judgment Hashr. Over 35 times in the Quran, Allah SWT references Al-Hashr. Allah SWT says, "Know that you will be gathered in front of him". So, there are many verses in the Quran.

Of them is one that links the Hashr with the trumpet immediately. In surah Taha verse 102, Allah Subhana WA Ta'ala says, "The day that the trumpet will be blown and we will then gather them on that day". So, the Hasher will come right after blowing of the Trumpet.

The Rain

The Hasher will begin with a gentle and persistent rain. It is going to rain for Allah SWT knows how long. The Prophet SAW said in a hadith in Sahih Muslim, "Then Allah will send down rain as if it is a cloud or a mound; and from this water, the bodies will grow back and become full again".

Water was used to create us. Allah SWT says in the Quran that water was used in our initial creation, and it will then be used in the second creation as well. In one hadith which is slightly weak it says, "Allah SWT will send water to the earth; and that water will come from under the throne of Allah Subhana WA Ta'ala".

It will be a water that is of a divine source. It will then cause mankind to grow out back as they were. It will cause mankind to come forth from their graves. The bodies will be recreated with that water coming down and the sand that they were in or the soil that they were in. Just like we were first created from the combination of water and sand.

Allah SWT says in the Quran that, "We created man from water and we created man from Turab". Turab is dry sand mixed with to feature like muddy water, and then hardened. That it reverberates.

The water will then cause the bodies to come out of the graves. This is explicitly referenced in the Quran multiple times perhaps. The most explicit one is by using the phrase Ba'athara. Which is mentioned at least three or four times in the Quran. It means the earth is turning over and shaking. So, when the person is going to come out of his grave, the earth that is around him will be shaking.

Allah SWT says in the Quran, "From this you were created. From sand and clay and water. And we're going to return you to this. Then we shall cause you to come out one more time from the same creation". This shows us that the bodies will be recreated. Obviously, our actual physical bodies will become dust. They're going to perish. Then Allah SWT will recreate the bodies.

Allah SWT says, "Like we created you in the beginning, we shall recreate you again". Allah SWT also says in the Quran, "we created the creation once in the beginning and then we shall do it all over again. And it will be even easier for him".

People Coming out of Their Graves

As the people come out of their graves, we learn that they will come out in different manners. One thing will be the same in all of them. Our Prophet SAW said, and the hadith is Sahih Bukhari and Muslim that, "When they will be resurrected, they will come out of their graves not wearing any shoes, naked without any clothes, uncircumcised. The way that you were originally first created. But you won't be a baby. you're going to be a fully grown person".

When Prophet SAW said this, Ayesha RA said, "Ya Rasool Allah, the men and the women will be naked? Won't they be staring at one another?" The Prophet SAW said, "O daughter of As Siddique, the matter is much more terrifying than that". Meaning for instance, when there's a tsunami wave coming, you're not going to be worried about these things. When the genuine terror strikes, may Allah protect us; that an earthquake is happening, you are not concerned about anybody else.

That is what Prophet SAW is saying that the matter is much more terrifying that people are not going to be caring about anybody else. Nobody cares what anybody else will be looking like or wearing.

The Prophet SAW told us in an authentic hadith that, "The first person to be resurrected is me. I will be the first person to come out of the grave". So, out of all of the creation our Nabi SAW will be the first to stand up. He said in another hadith that, "The first person to be clothed is Ibrahim AS".

The general rule is that everybody will be resurrected barefoot, naked and uncircumcised. But there are other Hadith of our Prophet SAW, where he authentically said a number of times, in a number of scenarios, that; for example, "Bury the Shaheed in his clothes. Because he shall be resurrected and the blood will be smelling like Musk".

When the Prophet SAW was going for Hajj, one of the Hujjaj, his camel jumped vertically on two legs, and the Hujjaj fell down on his head and he died. So, the Prophet SAW said, "Bury him in his Ihram, for he will be resurrected in that state, pronouncing the Talbiyah. Labaik Allahuma Labaik".

The opinion of the scholars is that they will all be resurrected naked, but the clothes that they will be given will be these clothes of the dunya. In this dunya, their clothes might have been cheap, but in the Akhira they will be a badge of honor. In the Akhira when all of mankind is naked and only the Muslims will be given clothes, and if somebody in Iharam on the day of judgment, obviously that's going to be a sign of Honor. Allah SWT is honoring him with that on this day.

Honor and Humiliation

Now the hadith tell us and the Quran tells us that some people will be resurrected in a manner that will either honor them or humiliate them. The actual resurrection itself when they come out of their graves, either immediately or shortly after that, things will happen to them that will either dishonor them or will raise their ranks.

For example, Allah SWT mentions in the Quran that, "certain groups of people, they're going to be resurrected on their faces". So, rather than standing up there will be upside down. The Prophet SAW was asked, the hadith is in Sahih Bukhari, "How can they be resurrected upside down?" Our Prophet SAW said "Isn't the one who caused them to walk standing capable of causing them to walk on their faces?"

Our scholars say that these people are getting this humiliation for refusing to bow their heads in Sajda in this dunya. We have a rule in the Sharia that the punishment will be in accordance with the crime you committed. The groups of people who were too arrogant to bow their heads to Allah SWT, they will be punished by being resurrected upside down.

Allah SWT mentions the Quran that, "On that day they will be resurrected on their faces being dragged to Jahannam". Our Prophet SAW mentions, "The one who caused them to walk standing, can cause them to be dragged upside down".

In another hadith in Tirmidhi, our Prophet SAW said that, "Those that had pride, they will be resurrected like atoms on the day of judgment". Of course, Atom is a modern word. The Arabic work used in Haith is Zerah. Meaning the smallest object imaginable. There's nothing smaller than that.

The Prophet SAW continued saying, "And people will trample over them. and People will say who are these individuals that are like Atoms? And it will be said to them these were the Prideful people in Dunya".

So, the punishment will begin from the very time of Resurrection. The punishment will begin from the time the graves open up and the bodies come out. Not all bodies are going to be the same. We learn this in a number of traditions.

In Sahih Muslim, our Prophet SAW said about the one who constantly asks people for favors for no reason; the one who keeps on asking people give him some money, and he doesn't have a need. He is not who's starving. He is someone who has no shame, no decency. The one who gets favors upon favors and he doesn't care about paying them back. He just wants to benefit from other people.

Our Prophet SAW said that, "A person will continue to ask people without any reason just taking advantage of others generosity; until he will come on the day of judgment and his whole face will be shredded, with not a single piece of flesh on it. His face will be like a bare skeleton".

In fact, this is mentioned in one statement of one of the Sahabah that, "A person who is rich but continues to ask people without a need, his face will be torn apart. His face will be shredded. He will have no dignity".

There are positive examples as well. The most obvious positive example is that our Prophet SAW said that, "The martyrs will be resurrected and their wounds will be as you see it. Its color will be the color of blood. But its smell will be the smell of musk. The smell will be of Jannah". Tt will be a badge of honor, that will impress the people around.

Another hadith mentions, "Every person shall be resurrected doing what they die doing". Another interpretation says, "Doing what they constantly did". So, the one who constantly did Zikr, or the one who constantly did some good deed, they will be resurrected and they will be doing that deed.

The one who did something evil, they will be doing the mechanisms of that evil, in a manner that will be dishonorable for them on the day of judgment.

We also know that the one who used to give the Azan, on the day of judgment he will be giving the Azan. According one narration, they are going to be recognized. Everybody will be looking up to them. It's translated as having longest necks on the day of judgment. Which is an expression.

Some of our scholars said that, the one who would be drinking alcohol when he died, he will be resurrected with the cup of alcohol in his hand. The people will see that this was a drunkard. We seek Allah SWT's refuge.

Righteous will be Clothed

Now the hadith explicitly mentions that people will be resurrected naked barefoot and uncircumcised. There is no exception for this. Then some people will be clothed. Please note that not all people will be clothed. The righteous will be clothed, and they will be clothed in accordance with their righteousness.

The first to be clothed will be the Prophets AS. Out of all of the Prophets AS, our Prophet SAW said, and the hadith is in Muslim, that, "I am the undisputed leader of all of the children of Adam AS on the day of judgment. And I'm not boasting. I'm just telling you because you need to know this. And I'm the first that the grave will open up for, and the body will come out".

He didn't have to say that he not boasting, but that is his modesty. The first grave that will open after the trumpet is blown is the grave in Medina of our Prophet SAW. The first human head to come out and the first body to be resurrected will be the body of our Prophet SAW.

Then he says something very interesting. Hadith is Sahih Bukhari. He said, "The first to be clothed on the day of judgment is Ibrahim AS". Now, he SAW is the first to come out. This might be in milliseconds. We would assume no other human would see the aura of the

Prophets AS. This is an assumption that we make. Because the Prophets AS are protected.

So, out of all the Prophets AS that are going to come out, instantaneously they will be clothed; and within a fraction of a millisecond. And the first to be clothed, the Prophet SAW said, "It's not me. It is my father Ibrahim AS".

Our scholars interpreted the reason for this is that, before Ibrahim AS was thrown in the fire, he was humiliated by being stripped naked and paraded in front of his people as a humiliation. So, to honor him on judgement day, in accordance with the effort he put in, he will be clothed first.

The one who was tortured in a way, the one who had to undergo suffering, their reward will be proportional, and we'll be in the same genre as their suffering. In this dunya if Ibrahim AS was humiliated in a certain manner, Allah SWT will honor him in the exact opposite manner. Of course, the Prophets AS will be resurrected first and then of course everybody will come after.

Jinns and Animals

We also know that the jinn will be resurrected. But we have no explicit hadith about how they will be. Because we do not know the bodies of the jinns, or the essence of the jinns. But they will obviously be resurrected because the Quran is very explicit that, "You will all be resurrected on the day of judgment".

Now what about animals and the other species? Will they be resurrected or not? Or will only the Jinn and the Humans be the one to be resurrected? One group of scholars have said that animals will not be resurrected. However, this appears to be an opinion that goes against explicit verses in the Quran and a hadith of the Prophet of Allah SAW.

Allah Azza Wajal says in the Quran, "When the wild beast will be resurrected". So even the beasts and the animals and the ants and the insects; everything that ever had a Ruh will be resurrected on the day of judgment.

Allah SWT says in the Quran, "There is not a single walking beast on this earth, nor even a bird in the heavens, except that they have civilizations like you. We haven't left anything out of this book. And then, on the day of judgment they will all be resurrected in front of their Lord".

This is explicit in the Quran. Now, why will the animals be resurrected? What is the purpose of animals being resurrected? Animals do not have heaven and hell. However, our Prophet SAW explained to us why animals will be resurrected. It's because animals will be resurrected to make sure that justice is met even amongst the other creations of Allah Azza Wajal.

How? It's not our concern, or our knowledge. But justice will be demonstrated on that day, even to animals. Because Allah Azza WA JAL is the ultimate one who is just. Allah SWT does not allow Zulm to happen and to go unchecked. This should send shivers down the spine of anyone who does Zulm to any other being.

If Allah SWT will not even allow an animal to get away with injustice, how then a human will for what he did to another human? Even an animal that unjustly attacks or harms another animal, on Judgment Day they will have to answer to Allah SWT within their mechanism.

We do not know how, because there is no heaven and hell for the animals. There's no legal responsibility for the animals. Yet, somehow justice will be meted out. This hadith is in Sahih Muslim, that our Prophet SAW said that, "Wallaahi, by Allah SWT, every single creation will argue with others on the day of judgement".

Meaning everybody will be suing everybody else that they knew, to try to get good deeds. Everyone will try to get whatever they can from anyone else. They're going to be very desperate.

Then he SAW said, "Until even two goats that butted against one another with their horns, the one that had full horns and the one that didn't. The one that didn't, will complain that this one attacked me. Because it was not fair that it attacked me. We're not an equal footing. This is Zulm".

Now, does this mean that the gazelle will complain to Allah SWT that the lion ate it? No, because this is not injustice. Allah Azza WA JAL has created this mechanism and checks and balances. The lion has the Haqq to go hunt the gazelle in the Sharia of Allah Azza WA Jal.

But there is Zulm that takes place even within the animal kingdom. The animals know what they should and should not do. Therefore, the Prophet SAW gives this example of the two goats; and Allah Azza WA Jal will deal with that on the day of judgement. No injustice will go unchecked on that day, even between animals.

We also know that in the hadith it is mentioned that after the animals' Hisab is done, they shall then be returned to dust. When the kafir sees the animals dissolving and disappearing, the kafir will say, which is in the Quran that, "They got out of the punishment of Allah SWT. How I wish that I was an animal". This clearly demonstrates that the animals will also be resurrected.

Resurrected without Senses

Now, we also learn that some people will be resurrected and their senses will be taken away from them. Some will be deaf, some will be dumb, some will be blind, and some will be all three. This is very explicit in the Quran that, Allah SWT says in Surah Al Israr verse 98 that, "On that day we shall resurrect them on their faces, deaf, dumb and blind".

Of course, in the famous verse in Surah Taha Allah SWT says that, "We shall resurrect him on the day of judgement blind. he will say, 'o Allah, I am blind now. But in the Dunia I used to be seeing. Why did you take my sight away?' Our signs came to you and you rejected and neglected them".

Meaning Allah SWT will reply to the person that, 'You saw the clear evidences for the existence of Allah SWT. You should have worshipped Allah SWT. But you rejected them. You didn't use your sight in the dunia, so of what use is it to you in the hereafter?'

Now this will not happen to all disbelievers. But some of them will be punished in this manner. Who? Allah knows best. Now, the Quran here mentions that they're going to be deaf, dumb and blind. Yet the Quran also mentions that they will see the fire of hell. It is because, all of the mankind will see Jahannam.

One of the leaders of Kharijites asked Ibn Abbas RA about these to Ayahs. He questioned him on how to reconcile between these two verses. Ibn Abbas RA said, "Wo to you. The day of judgment is going to be a very long day, and there will be many stations of that day. At one time, they will not speak, another time they will speak. One time they will swear and deny. At another time, their bodies will swear and deny. Their bodies will testify. At one time they will be blind, and another time they will see".

In other words, Judgment Day is not just a 10-minute ordeal. It will be a very, very, very long time. In fact, the day of judgement will feel like multiple lifetimes of our earthly existence to large groups of people. For the one who is going to be punished, there's going to be different types of punishment at different intervals of times.

He will try to argue with Allah SWT, then his mouth will be sealed, and the body will testify. At times he will be blind. At times he can see. All of these things are not going to happen at the same time.

People will Recognize Prophets AS

Another thing we learn as well is, on the day of judgment, people will somehow recognize the Prophets AS. Somehow, they will have a perception, that even without having seen these Prophets AS, they will know who they are.

We know this from the hadith in Bukhari and Muslim that, on the day of judgment, people will begin to gather. This is after being in the judgment day for a long time. That many lifetimes have gone by. Then they will want to move on. So, they will go to Adam AS. They will know who Adam AS is.

How? Allah SWT will give them that perception. Then they will go to Nuh AS, then Ibrahim AS. Then they will go to Musa AS, and then Isa AS, who will tell them to go to our Prophet SAW.

Ard al-Mahshar

So, after the resurrection is going to take place, the Hasher is going to happen. Then the gathering will come. After this, the next stage is called Al-Mawqif. The next stage is the land of Al-Hasher. Where will Al Hasher take place? Where is the gathering of the people going to be?

The Mawqif is explicitly referred to in the Quran and in the Sunnah concept wise. Allah SWT says in the Quran, in surah Ibrahim verse 48, "On that day the earth will be substituted for another earth and the heavens for another heavens".

Allah SWT is saying that the land of the judgement day is a totally different land. This land is not something you are familiar with. Now some reports mention that the Mawqif will take place in the valleys of Arafat. These narrations are authentic. It is because perhaps the land of Arafat will be transformed to this new land.

Allah SWT says in the Quran judgement day is the day that the earth shall be transformed to another earth. There is a transformation taking place. Which means there was something in the beginning, and there's something in the end. The resurrection will occur in the plains of Arafat. That's in one narration from the Sahabah.

So, perhaps the lands and planes of Arafat will be changed to this other earth. In the hadith in Bukhari, our Prophet SAW said, "Allah SWT will roll up the earth and he shall roll up the heavens in his right hand. And he will say, 'I am the king. Where are the kings of this world?'"

Here the world and the heavens being rolled up means that they will be put aside. They're not going to be the next earth. For the next earth, our Prophet SAW gave us one description. One hadith that is explicit. This hadith is in Buhari. He SAW says, "The people shall be resurrected on the day of judgement upon a land that is pure white, unblemished. Without any spot on it. Like sifted wheat. And it is all on the ground. There's not going to be any flag, or any mountain, or any hill or any markings that are going to tell one part from another".

Some of the Sahaba described the Land of Assembly as being like silver. A pure land upon which no sin has ever been committed. In other words, the land of the Mahshar is flat. It is stretching as far as the eye can see. Wherever you see, there will be no mark, no hill, no flag. Nothing to tell where you are, versus where other people are. As far as the eye can see, everything will look exactly the same.

There's will be no way to tell where you are positioned. This is something that is very strange for us. It hardly ever happens to any of us. Even if you are in the desert, you will see a mountain there. You will see something there to situate you.

It is as if, for people who go deep in the oceans, and when they are surrounded by water as far as the eye can see; they feel some palpitation. Everything is exactly the same under the ocean. It is completely unrecognizable from point A to point B.

Therefore, how will we find one another? Our Prophet SAW said, and hadith is in Bukhari and Muslim that, "Allah SWT will gather all of the creation in one land. The one who calls out, will be heard by all. And the one who wants to see, will be able to see all".

In other words, if you want to call out to somebody, somehow your voice will reach that person. If you want to see somebody amongst hundreds of billions of people, you will be able to see them. How will it happen? Allah SWT knows best. But if you want to get your haq from somebody, that person will not be able to hide.

Anybody who wants to call you, anybody who wants to complain against you, anyone who wants to put his lawsuit in this judgment of Allah SWT against you, they will be able to find you.

We also learn from the Sunnah, and the Quran references it indirectly that the Sun will come close to the day of judgment, and the creation we'll be in a state of anxiety and fear, dealing with the terror on that day.

There are dozens of verses in the Quran Some of them are explicit and powerful. In Surah Ibrahim verses 42, Allah SWT says, "Do not think that Allah is unaware of what the wrongdoers are doing". Don't think Allah SWT is not aware of what is happening around the world. Don't think Allah SWT is unaware of the ones killing and plundering and causing people's lives to be disrupted. Don't ever assume that these people will be let go.

Allah SWT continues, "Allah is going to delay them to the day when the eyes will be staring in a glaze". Notice how Allah SWT is describing. When do your eyes stare in a glaze? It is when you are terrified. When you're terrified, you don't blink. Everybody is going to be staring. Everybody is going to be in a state of fear. Except for people that Allah SWT has protected.

Then Allah SWT says, "Their necks will be outstretched. They will be wondering what is going to happen next. Their heads are raised up. Their eyelids are not even blinking. And their hearts are empty in their chests. They don't feel their heart". Meaning the palpitation is so much, they feel empty in the heart. notice this graphic description. This is the default of mankind. Allah SWT is saying this is how people are going to be.

Allah SWT also says in the Quran in Surah Nisa verse 42 that, "On that day those who rejected the Prophet SAW, they would wish that the earth destroys them. They would want the earth to swallow them up. And Allah SWT will not conceal anything".

In the hadith of Sahih Bukhari, The Prophet SAW says, "The Sun will come close to the creation on the day of judgment until it will be the distance of a **meal**".

One of the narrators of the hadith, he said, "Wallaahi, I don't know what **meal** means. Does he SAW mean mile of the earth, or does he mean the dip". So, another meaning for meal in classical Arabic was thing that you put into the bottle. We call it the silver dip. Besides, Allah SWT knows best what it actually means.

The Prophet SAW continues, "Then people will begin to sweat in accordance with their deeds". Meaning in accordance with how pious or sinful they are. So, the more sinful person will feel more palpitation and will be more nervous and will sweat more.

The Prophet SAW said, "For some of them, the sweat will only go to their ankles. Others will go to their shins. Others will come to their chests. Yet others, it will drown them completely in their sweat, by coming up to their mouth".

As we already mentioned, people will be resurrected in different manners and the punishment will begin. But the safety mechanisms will also begin. Allah SWT says in the Quran, "And the righteous, on that day shall be protected from the terror". This is very explicit. So that terror that will happen, if we are truly righteous, we will not face that terror.

Duration of Judgment Day

Now, how long will the day of judgment be? There are three verses in the Quran that Ulema believe answer this question. It is mentioned in Surah al-Hajj verse 47, "And the day in the sight of your lord is like a thousand years of your reckoning". This verse is saying that, obviously, for Allah SWT time is not like what it is for us.

Our concept of time is different. Allah SWT created time. Time is a creation of Allah SWT. Time is a Makhluk. It is one of the Makhluk of Allah SWT that our minds cannot fully understand and comprehend.

Allah SWT says in Surah Al-Ma'arij verse 4, "The Angels will come up to him and Jibreel AS as well; on a day that shall be as long as fifty thousand years".

Also, Allah SWT says in Surah Sajda verse 5, "He is the one who controls and monitors what happens in the heavens and the earth. And then, there shall be an ascent on the day that will be a thousand years of your reckoning".

Now, the question arise, one verse says fifty thousand years, other says one thousand. Do both of these verses apply to the day of judgment? We do not know.

Ibn Abbas RA was asked about these two verses. He said, "I don't know. Two days that Allah SWT has mentioned in the Quran, I believe in both of them. I don't know if they are the same or they are different." It is because the verses don't explicitly say that they are talking about the day of judgment.

Some Ulema have said that, the day of judgment will be one thousand years of your time frame. Our average life span that we are actually physically awake is around 40 to 50 years. Actual lifespan is 70 to 80 years. But in terms of activity, it is 40 to 50 years. The day of judgment will be multiple lifetimes. But it will feel like fifty thousand years. So, one thousand actual years and it will feel like fifty thousand years. This is one interpretation.

Another interpretation is that, it will be one thousand for one group of people and up to fifty thousand for another group of people. With some people in between as well.

Another interpretation is that, the thousand-year reference is not about day of judgment. It is about the length of time that it takes for the Angels to go up to Allah Subhanahu Wa'ta'ala; and the day of judgment will be fifty thousand years. So out of the two verses, one doesn't apply to the Judgment Day, and one of them does.

In the end of the day, we say what Ibn Abbas RA said, "I don't know". And Allah SWT knows best. But there is clearly some evidence to indicate relativity of judgement day. There is clearly evidence to indicate that some people will feel judgment is quicker than others.

Of them, Allah SWT says in the Quran, "The day of judgement will be a very difficult day for the kafir". In another verse, Allah SWT says, "That is a very difficult day. it will not be easy for the kafir". Now, Allah SWT is saying, it won't be easy for the kafir. What is the implication? It will be easy for the believer.

If it was difficult for the believer, why would Allah SWT specify? This is the derived meaning of these Ayahs. Allah SWT doesn't explicitly say that it will be easy for the Muslims.

Also, the hadith in Musnad Imam Ahmed, in which our Prophet SAW said, "I swear by the one in whose hands is my soul, the day of judgment will be easier for the believer. So much so that, it will be lighter for him and quicker for him, then the obligatory prayers that he will pray in this dunya".

The obligatory prayer of 4 Rakat takes five to seven minutes. It will be easier for the believer than that obligatory Salah. For the righteous believer, day of judgment is just a formality. It might be a thousand years, but Allah Azza WA JAL will allow the believer to zoom through that.

Also, the hadith of Prophet SAW that says, "For the believer, Qiyamah will be like the time between Zohar and Asr". In another version, it says "between Asr and Maghrib". So, there are two or three hours between Zohar and Asr and some hour and a half between Asr and Maghrib. So, it will feel like something quick.

There is one more evidence that does seem to suggest that the 50,000 does apply to the day of judgment. It is a hadith that is in Bukhari and Muslim. It is narrated by Abu Huraira RA. Our Prophet SAW said that, "Anyone who owns gold or silver, and does not pay zakat on it; that zakat will be turned into a fire that will be used to burn him, and his body, on his face, and his sides; in a day that shall stretch to fifty thousand years. Then he will see whether he's going to heaven or hell".

This hadith is very explicit, that states the maximum amount of time for the day of judgement. Whether it is real or whether it is perception, we don't know. But we can conclude that the day of judgment will maximum be felt for 50,000 years.

Now think about it. 50,000 years, that is an eternal lifetime. That's why people will become so exasperated, that they will even be willing to go on to Jahannam, so that judgment day will finish.

Descriptions of the Day of Judgement

There is a famous Hadith of the Prophet SAW, reported in Tirmidhi. Our Prophet SAW said, "Whoever wants to see the day of judgment in Vivid detail as if you are looking at it, let him read Surah Al Takweer and let him read Surah Al-Infitar". Therefore, we should especially go over these two Surahs for the day of judgment.

We are going to briefly go over the translation. Allah SWT says in Surah Al Takweer, "When the sun is rolled up. And when the stars are diminished and extinguished. And when the mountains are moving in motion. And when all relationships will be broken and suspended. And when all of the animals will be gathered together. And when the oceans will become flames. When the oceans themselves are set a light with fire. And when souls are paired up. And when the baby child that was killed is going to be asked why was she killed. And when the scrolls are spread out and everybody can read them. And when the sky is peeled away. When the fire is set Ablaze and Jannah is brought close. On that day every soul will have in front of him what that soul prepared for the day of judgment. Every soul can see this is what I prepared for the day of judgement".

Meaning on the day of Judgment the sun will collapse on itself, and it will not be there anymore. There will be no Stars anymore. The mountains will no longer be stabled. That what we think is the most stable will itself be moving. We think of water as extinguishing and Allah SWT is saying on the day of judgement it will be so hot, the water itself will become fire.

What we thought is going to extinguish the fires will itself become a source of heat. Every Zalim and Mazloum will be face to face, and you're not going to run out on that day. The girls that was buried alive, will be asked why she was buried alive. Scrolls that were kept hidden will be made open and public. The sky is going to collapse as we Know It. You will get your Hisab there. All your deeds will be in front of you.

Allah SWT says in Surah Al-Infitar that, "When the sky will split asunder. And when the planets are going to be scattered. When the oceans will explode. and the graves are going to be turned over. Every single soul shall know what it has brought forth and what it has left behind. O Mankind, why are you deceived about your generous Lord? What is deluding you from worshipping Allah SWT, the one who created you? He created you. He shaped you. And he gave you your proportion and your body. Rather you don't really believe in the day of judgment. You have Angels that are watching over you. There are noble writers Kiraman Katibin. They are knowing and writing what you are doing. They are not going to be absent on the day of judgment. But what will you understand about the day of judgement? What will convey to you what is the day of judgment? On that day, no soul shall help another soul. And every affair and decision will be made by Allah SWT".

Meaning on the day of judgment, the sky is going to crack open. You will not have the stability of the Skies. Because again one thing that is steady is the skies above us. Wherever we go, we see the skies. Wherever we go, there is land beneath us. Even the ocean is on the Earth. Even in an air plane, we see the land and we see the skies. But on the day of judgment, that which was most stable, will be completely gone.

Not just this world, all the planets around us and all of the stars will be gotten rid of. In the previous Surah it was mentioned that the oceans will be on fire, in this Surah Allah SWT says they will explode out. Every soul will know what they actually did and what opportunities they missed. Allah SWT created you in your shape. No soul shall be of any use to another soul.

Also, the last verse here, this is one of the primary descriptions of the day of judgment. In over half-a-dozen explicit versus Allah SWT keeps on reminding that in this dunya you have help. However, on the day of judgment every person will be by himself or herself.

There will be no ties of kinship, no friendship, no friends in powerful places.

Allah SWT says, "The people that are destined to go to Jahannam, they don't have a single friend that is going to help you. Not one person to intercede". Allah SWT says, "Even the closest of friends on that day they won't even ask about their friends".

Allah SWT says, "When the trumpet is blown, there will be no ties of kinship. They won't even ask about one another". All of your close friends and families all of those that you thought were your allies, on the day of judgment, will not care about anyone else. In fact, not only not care, but you will try to hide from those whom you knew and you took support and comfort from in this dunya.

Allah SWT says that, on that day, the person will run away from his own brother, from his own wife, from his own children, from his own mother, from his own father. Every single person is only worried about matters pertaining to himself.

We learn from all of this is that there will be a general sense of selfishness. Why would there not be? Because this is heaven and hell. You have to answer for yourself. The Quran is explicit that there will also be a moment or a long period of fear and introspection. That there will be a sense of trepidation. That will cause everybody, at least in the beginning of the day of judgement, to be completely quiet, terrified and confused. That will mean no one will speak.

This is again mentioned explicitly in the Quran. Allah SWT says, "When they come on that day, not a single soul will speak unless Allah SWT has given them permission to speak". There will be the Prophets AS who will speak, because Allah SWT has given them permission to speak. Everybody else will be quiet.

Allah SWT says in the Quran, "On that day the Ruh and Jibreel and the Angels are all standing in rows. No one will say one thing. Neither the Angels, nor the human beings. Except for those whom Allah SWT has given permission to speak. Then they will speak".

Allah SWT says in Surah Taha versus 108, "On that day all sounds will be silent in front of Rehman. Every voice is going to go quiet. You will only hear shuffling of feet as they go to the day of judgement". It means the mumblings that we say, but nobody can hear you. You're trembling. You want to say something. But sound is not even coming out. It is a voice that is so small. Even the person standing next to you cannot understand.

Our Prophet SAW said, the hadith is in Bukhari, "On that day, no one will speak except for the Prophets of Allah". They will be the ones who will break that silence, when Allah SWT allows them to break the silence.

Concept of Shafa'a

After the Mawqif, after the Hasher has come, after the souls have been gathered together, and they're in front of Allah SWT, and there is dead silence; the next thing that will take place will be the intersection of the Prophets SAW to begin the day of judgment.

Now, this intersection is a type of intersection. Because there are different types of intercessions. All of them will occur after the first one, that will be by Prophet SAW. So, we're going to take a deep dive into the concept of Shafa'a, and we're going to mention many categories of Shafa'a. There are many dozens of Ayahs and Hadiths about the concept of Shafa'a.

Now, what is the concept of Shafa'a? Shafa'a actually means 'to be even' in the linguistic manner. It means that you bring somebody to plead your case in front of a third-party. What has the concept of even to do with the concept of pleading your case in front of somebody else?

It is because when you bring the Intercessor, you become even from odd. This is the linguistic connotation of even, versus bringing somebody to intercede.

Now the Quran generally speaking, when it talks about Shafa'a, it always conditions Shafa'a. Allah SWT is praised by not allowing unconditional Shafa'a. This is something that is very unique. Because every human being without exception, they are people they need to please.

You might think, if you're powerful, then you get away with many things. But whoever is powerful, they still need to surround themselves with people of power and status, and have their protection. In order to have their protection, he needs to give them perks as well.

Every single person of wealth and power has an entourage, that he needs to be a person of wealth and power. Every King, every president has a group that they rely on. It doesn't matter who you are, you as an individual cannot do anything without the help of others. And the people who are doing that help, they need perks from you. Same way you need perks from them. Hence when one of them comes to you for something, then you have to do what needs to be done.

There is only one who has no need of any help or intercessor. That is Allah SWT. Allah SWT affirms that no one can give Shafa'a in front of him, unless he allows that person. This is something that is a constant theme of the Quran. Allah SWT mentions that, "Fear the day that no Shafa'a will help them on the day of judgement".

Similarly, right before Ayat Al-Kursi, Allah SWT says, "There won't be any Shafa'a on the day of judgement". Then in Ayat Al-Kursi Allah SWT asks a rhetorical question that, "Isn't it obvious? Who is there that can even try Shafa'a, much less have it accepted? Who is there that can even open his mouth for Shafa'a except if Allah SWT gives permission?"

In Surah Yunus verse 3, Allah SWT says, "There is no intercessor, except after Allah SWT has allowed". In Surah Al-Anbiya verse 28 Allah SWT says, "They cannot intercede accept on behalf of people whom Allah SWT is already pleased with. On that day no Shafa'a will be accepted except if Allah SWT has given permission and Allah SWT is pleased".

So, our Scholars mention that for any Shafa'a to occur on Judgment Day, two conditions must be met. Both of them are linked directly with Allah SWT.

The first condition is that Allah SWT will allow certain groups of people to intercede. They do not have the right to stand up and say, "Allah SWT I want this person to be saved". Rather, Allah SWT will give that person the opportunity if Allah SWT choses. No one has that privilege. It is not any right that anyone has. This is very explicit in the Quran.

To some people Allah SWT will give permission to go ahead and speak, and give them opportunity to make

Shafa'a. The righteous people will be the one will get this opportunity. Meaning the Angels, the Prophets AS, the Shaheed etc. Our Prophet SAW said, "The Martyr has 70 people he can make Shafa'a for". In one Hadith in Tirmidhi, Prophet SAW says that, "The Hafiz has 10 people that he can make Shafa'a for".

Our Prophet SAW said that, "There will be a person from my Ummah who will be able to make Shafa'a for more people than the number of people in tribe of Banu Tamim". Banu Tamim tribe is the largest of the Arab tribes. There are still, to this day, members of this tribe in the millions.

And the Prophet SAW said, "There's one person of my Ummah, Allah SWT will bless him to give Shafa'a to more people, than in the entire tribe of Banu Tamim". Our Prophet SAW said that, "The child will make Shafa'a for its parents if it died". Every child that dies, and if the parents were righteous, the child will make Shafa'a for them.

So, this is the first condition that Allah SWT will allow a person. And in some Hadith, we learn that they will be given a quota. They can have 17 or 70, or unlimited. The second condition is that their Shafa'a will not be accepted unless Allah SWT is pleased with the people on whose behalf, they're asking intersection.

This condition is explicit in the Quran, that just because Allah SWT gives you the permission to make Shafa'a; it does not mean that Shafa'a will be accepted. This is explicit in the Quran. Allah SWT describes that there are countless Angels in the heavens and the earth. Allah SWT has given them the permissibility to makes Shafa'a. There Shafa'a will be of no value except after Allah SWT has accepted those whom he chooses.

These are the two conditions that are explicit in the Quran for a Shafa'a to be effective. Allah SWT is going to allow one group of people to make Shafa'a on behalf of other group of people. Then Allah SWT will pick and choose whoever he wants in the end.

Now, why did Allah SWT assign a specific number of Shafa'a for a certain group of people, knowing that in the end of the day, Allah will accept Shafa'a for some of them and reject for some of them. Meaning Allah SWT has assigned a Martyr 70 people, be he can accept 35 and reject remaining 35.

The reason is that Allah SWT is honoring one group of people by allowing them to speak and make Shafa'a, on a day when no one speaks. At a time when everybody is trembling, the honor is that not only have you passed the exam, Allah SWT has given you permission to try to bring some other people out.

Is it not an honor that when the majority of mankind are trembling, sitting down, one person will stand up and he will have a chance of getting 70 people with him to Jannah?

Now obviously, the one who will get it, is the one who deserves that honor. Therefore, the more righteous a person is, the more likelihood is that they will be given a quantity. And the higher their Iman, the more the quantity will be.

Is it not the means of honor that one person can make Shafa'a for as many people as the population of the tribe of Banu Tamim? That one person can make Shafa'a for millions of people at once?

This one person is from the Ummah of the Prophet SAW. That one person is not a Prophet. It is somebody lesser than the Prophets AS. The Prophets AS will have even more. What do you think? Is this not an honor even if 60% of his Shafa'a are accepted and 40% are rejected?

Now, as for those that are forgiven in the end, Allah SWT is using the mechanism of Shafa'a to forgive them, knowing they would be forgiven. Allah SWT uses many mechanisms. This is one of the mechanisms that he's using.

That is why Hassan Al Basri RA said, "Increase the number of your righteous friends. For Allah SWT knows, whose Shafa'a will be accepted". Don't hang around those who are going to drag you down. Don't hang around those that are bad influence on you. Don't hang around those who are casting Akhlaq issues on to you. Find righteous company. So that, even if maybe you don't quite make it, may Allah SWT protect us; but if you were with the righteous, maybe they will be your way to Jannah.

As the famous scholar said, "I love the righteous, even if even if I'm not amongst them. Maybe their piety will rub off on me and maybe on Judgment Day, one of their Shafa'a will come for me as well".

Now, who will get to the Shafa'a? Think about it. Suppose somebody has been given 10 people to choose. Who will he choose? Those whom he owes favors to. Those that have an impact on him. So, in this, there's a reason for us to be good to other people. A reason for us to be generous. A reason for us to have good Akhlaq. To control your anger.

There are many Hadiths of this nature. Of them is that, there was a man who would do many sins. He would also loan money to people. But when the time came to collect the money, he would tell his servants, 'If they don't have the money, leave them be. Maybe Allah SWT will give me some ease on the day of judgement".

So, he comes on the day of judgment full of his sins, and Allah SWT says, "I have more right to show you mercy, than you had to give to them. Go ahead you forgiven". This is Shafa'a. Those people were impacted by his generosity. So, what is the wisdom of Shafa'a? Very obvious. Allah SWT will honor one group of people and Allah SWT will forgive another group through the mechanism of Shafa'a.

Butt in the end, the one who controls the Shafa'a is Allah SWT. We say this because, unfortunately, some Muslims have this notion that certain Makhluk of Allah SWT have the ultimate right to ask Allah SWT and be given what they demand. But this is not true. No matter how blessed a person might be, the person is a creation, and Allah SWT is the creator. So, we need to be very clear that Shafa'a is not a right.

Shafa'a of Prophet SAW

Now, as we said any righteous person can be given the ability to make Shafa'a by Allah SWT. Every righteous person has the potential. Every Angel can give Shafa'a. The Quran will give Shafa'a. The money you giving in charity will give Shafa'a on Judgment Day. The ground that you do sajda on might give Shafa'a. The whole Makhluk of Allah SWT have the potential to give Shafa'a if Allah SWT allows them.

Who will have the lion's share of Shafa'a? Obviously, our Prophet SAW. He will have the greatest quantity and the most variety and quality. This is understood. No doubt about it. So, we will now look at the Shafa'at of our Prophet SAW has. When you look at the Quran and the Sunnah, you find many Shafa'at of our Prophet SAW. Scholars differ on how many types of Shafa'a our Prophet SAW has.

Abu Bakr An Nakash RA says, "Our Prophet SAW has three types of Shafa'a. The general Shafa'a, the Shafa'a of the first batch that enter Jannah, and the Shafa'a for the major sinners".

Ibn Atiya RA from Andalus, in his Tafsir called "Tafsir Ibn Atiya", mentions that our prophet SAW has two categories of Shafa'a. The general Shafa'a and the Shafa'a to take people out of Jahannam and take them into Jannah. Then he says, The Shafa'a to take people out of Jahannam and take them to heaven is for all righteous people. So, first one is exclusive to Prophet SAW and the other is general.

Al Qa'deyat RA, another scholar from Andalus said that there will be 5 Shafa'at for the Prophet SAW. Number one the general Shafa'a. Number two, the people who will enter Jannah without Hisab. Number 3, some people are destined to go to Jahannam, the verdict has been given, but before they enter Jahannam, the Shafa'a of Prophet SAW saves them.

Number four, those who have entered Jahannam are allowed to exit before their time, because of the Shafa'a of the Prophet SAW. Number five is the Shafa'a of Darajat. It is the Shafa'a of Prophet SAW to raise the ranks of people higher than what they deserved. This is for people who got in Jannah, but at a lower level. Then with the Shafa'a of Prophet SAW, they will get in to a higher level of Jannah.

Ibn Kathir RA writes that there are eight Shafa'a of our Prophet SAW. Number one, the grand Shafa'a. Number two, the Shafa'a for people whose good and bad deeds were the same, but the Shafa'a will tilt in the side of the good deeds. Number 3, those who have been commanded to go to Jahannam, but before they get there, they will be saved. Number four, those who would be raised above with their level in Paradise.

Number five, those who will enter Jannah without Hisab. Number 6, the special Shafa'a that he will do for his uncle Abu Talib. Number 7, The Shafa'a for the people of Jannah to enter Jannah.

People will not be able to enter Jannah until our Prophet SAW make Shafa'a for them to enter Jannah. No one will enter Jannah until our Prophet SAW make Shafa'a for the gates of Jannah to open. Then the gates of Jannah will open. Number 8 is for the major sinners of the Muslim Ummah.

Categories of Shafa'a

Now, some of the categories of Shafa'a that we mentioned above are unique to our Prophet SAW. For example, opening the gates of Jannah and the grand Shafa'a. But others are open to many other categories of people. For example, saving people from Jahannam. This is the default meaning of Shafa'a.

When a Martyr is asked to make Shafa'a he will not be choosing a person already going to Jannah. He will choose the person who are destined to Jahannam. As, on the day of judgment, Allah SWT has given him.

Also, the ability to make Shafa'a for a person at lower level of Jannah to go to a higher level of Jannah is given to every single person of Jannah. Every single person of Jannah is allowed to adjust position of their loved ones within Jannah. Meaning, a person at a higher level of Jannah can make Shafa'a for his loved ones that are at a lower level of Jannah to be moved to that same level.

There is a Hadith that, a man came to Prophet SAW and said, "Ya Rasool Allah SAW, I don't have much good deeds. But I love Allah SWT and his Messenger SAW". The Prophet SAW said, "You will be with those whom you love".

No one will be deprived of his or her family and friends in Jannah. It is in the Quran. Allah SWT says, "Those that did good, then their progeny did good after them, we shall match them up with their progeny and have them together".

The Grand Shafa'a

The first category is the Grand Shafa'a or Shafa'a At Ul-Uzma in Arabic. Majority of Scholars say that the Grand Shafa'a is the same thing as Maqam Al Mahmood. Maqam Al Mahmood is mentioned in the Quran once very explicitly.

It is mentioned in Surah Isra. Allah SWT says, "Pray Tahajud Ya Rasool Allah SAW, perhaps Allah SWT will resurrect you in the Maqam Al Mahmood". Therefore, after the Azan is called, we make a dua. In that dua we ask Allah SWT to grant Prophet SAW the Maqam Al Mahmood and to resurrect him on the Maqam Al Mahmood. So, Maqam Al Mahmood is pertaining to resurrection and it is explicitly linked to the day of judgement.

Now, the majority of Ulema believe that Maqam Al Mahmood is the same thing as the Grand Shafa'a. But there are other opinions about the Grand Shafa'a and Maqam Al Mahmood as well. Now Maqam means a station. Mahmood means praiseworthy. So, Maqam Al Mahmood is a station that is a praiseworthy station, that people are thanking and praising.

One opinion is that Maqam Al Mahmood is that the Prophet SAW will be given the flag and the banner of mankind on the day of judgement. Only one person will carry it to represent Mankind, and this flag is called the flag of praise. So, the one who is carrying the banner of praise, is being given the station of praise.

The evidence is that, there's a Hadith in Tirmidhi, that the Prophet SAW said, "I shall be the leader of the children of Adam and I don't say this out of Pride. I shall be the leader on the day of judgment. And in my hand shall be the banner of praise. And I'm not saying this out of arrogance. And every Prophet including Adam AS and all who come after him will be under my banner. And I'll be the first who will get out of the grave. And I say this without any arrogance".

So, in this Hadith 4 things are mentioned, and each time the Prophet SAW is clarifying that we need to know that this is the Maqam that Allah SWT has given him. So, on the day of judgment there's going to be something called The Flag of Praise, and some scholars have said that is Maqam Al Mahmood.

Another group of scholars have said that the Maqam Al Mahmood is that he shall be the one who knocks on the door of Jannah. The Hadith is in Musnad Imam Ahmed that the Prophet SAW said, "I shall be the first person to knock on the doors of Jannah, and Jannah will not open to anybody else". The first person to step in Jannah with his right foot, will be our Prophet SAW.

So according to some scholars this is Maqam Al Mahmood as everybody's going to praise him for opening the doors of Jannah.

Another opinion of is that the Maqam Al Mahmood is that Allah SWT will take the Prophet SAW and place him next to him on the throne. This interpretation was the position of some of the classic Ulema. But there is no evidence of this from the Quran and Sunnah.

Now as per the majority of the scholars, Shafa'a Al Ul Uzma is called the Grand Shafa'a because there is no Shafa'a that is more important than it. That's why it's called the most honorable Shafa'a. No Shafa'a is greater than it. What it means is that it will be the Shafa'a for the day of judgment to begin.

The reason why it will be called Maqam Al Mahmood is that every single Makhluk, without exception, will thank the Prophet SAW for doing and causing the Shafa'a by the permission of Allah SWT. Every Jinn and Human will thank our Prophet SAW and will praise him, because he was the one whose Shafa'a allowed to begin the proceedings of judgment day.

Because as it was explained earlier, that Judgment day is going to be a long time. There will be a sense of chaos and a sense of fear and a sense of trepidation. That people will not know what to do. In that frustration, some will even say, "Let judgment happen, even if we go to Jahannam. It is better than this period of weight".

So, they're going to be in such a long state that all of mankind will just want judgment to begin. So that they can move on to the next stage. Whatever the next stage might be. And to make that judgment to begin, they will go to various people, to see who will be the one who can go speak to Allah SWT on behalf of all creation.

That is why Maqam Al Mahmood is not just the one who opens the doors of Jannah. Maqam Al Mahmood is Shafa'a Al Ul Uzma, because every Makhluk, without exception will thank our Prophet SAW, and we'll choose our Prophet SAW, and will honor our Prophet SAW. Allah SWT has honored him by giving it to him. And all of the creation will unanimously choose one person to represent them.

It is because Shafa'a At Ul Uzma is the beginning of everything. After it the Mizan will be brought down. After it, Allah SWT will come with the Angels. After it the Hisab is done. Nothing is happening until Shafa'a At Ul Uzma. It is the first step before the other steps of judgment day.

The most famous Hadith about this Shafa'a of Maqam Al Mahmood is a Hadith that is in Bukhari and Muslim. It is one of the longest hadith and it is very beneficial. This Hadith is narrated by Anas Ibn Malik RA. The Prophet

Said, "Allah SWT will gather the believers on the day of judgement in the same way that they are gathered in this life. And the people will say, let us find someone to make Shafa'a for us in front of Allah SWT. So that we can move on from the terrors of today".

The Hadith is indicating that a long time will come and that long time will make the people to start feeling agitated and nervous. They want to move on to the next stage no matter what the next stage is. So, they're going to hunt for one person who will then go in front of Allah SWT and make Shafa'a.

One of them will say "Let us go to Adam AS". So, they will all say, "Yes, let us all go to Adam AS". Then mankind will come to Adam AS and they will say to Adam AS that, "oh Adam AS don't you see the situation, we are all in right now? You are our father. You are the one whom Allah SWT created with his two hands and Allah SWT ordered the Angels to prostrate. Allah SWT taught you the names of everything". They're praising their father Adam AS.

Then they will say, "You become our intercessor in front of our Lord. So that we may relieve ourselves from the terror of today". Adam AS will respond, "This is not for me. I'm not worthy of this, because I ate of the tree that I shouldn't have eaten from. I committed a mistake that I should not have done. Go to Nuh AS, as he was the first Rasool whom Allah SWT sent".

Adam AS was a Nabi, while Nuh AS was a Rasool. The people will then go to Nuh AS. They will praise him and give the praise that is deserving of him. But Nuh AS will say, "I am not worthy of this. I asked Allah SWT for something, when he forbade me to ask". Meaning when Allah SWT said, "Do not ask me about those that are not on your ship. If they choose your ship, they are safe. If they do not, don't ask about the wrong doers".

But Nuh AS said to Allah SWT, "O Allah, my son; you didn't save him". Allah SWT said, "He's not from real family". Now, Nuh AS feels guilty for disobeying Allah SWT in this regard. Then Nuh AS will say, "Go to the one whom Allah SWT chose as his special friend. Go to the Khalil of Allah SWT. Go to Ibrahim AS".

They will go to Ibrahim AS and they will praise him. But Ibrahim AS will say, "I am not worthy for I lied 3 times in my life, and I have to answer for those sins". But realize that all the sins the Prophets AS are worried for are utterly trivial. Nuh AS became emotional and he asked Allah SWT about his family. Now, he's feeling guilty that he asked Allah SWT.

Same way, Ibrahim AS did not technically lie. All of these three things that he said they are called double meaning or double entendre. That it's not quite a lie. He was doing something that is for a greater good. Of the things that he is worried about is that, when the people came to abduct Sarah RA, and there were going to kill him if he was the husband of Sarah RA.

He said, "She is my sister". He meant my sister in Islam, and he said that to save his life. So, they left him alive, or else they would have killed him. Now, he is worried how he will answer Allah SWT that I said this. Imagine that terror in their Iman that has come, that they have to answer Allah SWT.

The second one is that, he said, "This bid Idol is the one who killed the other Idols"; when villagers asked him about the idols being broken. Because of that he is worried. It was a dawah opportunity. It was not meant to deceive. It was meant to make them think.

The third one was when he told the villagers, "I am not feeling well. Go without me". By the way, he was 14 years old at this time. He passed away at the age of 120. And Ibrahim AS is worried that he told his people, "I'm not feeling well. So, leave me in the city". So, that he can destroy the idols.

For this Ibrahim AS is saying, "I'm not worthy. Go to the one whom Allah SWT spoke with directly. Go to Musa AS". So, they will go to Musa AS. They will praise Musa AS. Musa AS will respond that, "I am not worthy. I killed an innocent man, when I had no right to kill him".

Now, again, realize that the killing was not even intentional. He punched him. he did not intend to do any significant harm to that man. it was a genuine mistake. Now, he is saying I have to answer for that. "I'm not worthy. Go to somebody else. Go to Isa AS.

So, mankind will go Isa AS. They will praise him. They will say that, "Allah SWT created you without a father". But Isa AS will say, "I am not worthy". The Prophet SAW said, "Isa AS will not mention any sin that he has done". There will be no sin even in his mind. And Isa AS was raised up at the age of 33. A very young man.

But he will be saying, "I'm not worthy. Go to somebody else. Go to Muhammad SAW". By the way, these are the five Ul Al Azam from The Messengers, along with our father Adam AS.

The last of them, will be our Prophet SAW. He is the last Prophet chronologically, but he is the highest in terms of status. They will go to the Prophet SAW, and they will praise him the way he is worthy of being praised. Then they will say, "Will you make Shafa'a for us in front of Allah SWT?"

The Prophet SAW will not send them anywhere. He will say, "This is my job". So, all of mankind will unanimously elect our Prophet SAW to represent them. The Muslim and the Kafirs; the men of them and the women of them; the humans and the Jinns; then everybody will Unanimously agree that the Prophet SAW represents them.

This is why it is called Al Maqam Al Mahmood. The praiseworthy station. Because all of mankind will praise him. So, he will go in front of Allah SWT.

The Prophet SAW said, "I will walk to the Throne and I will fall down in prostration in front of the Throne of Allah SWT. And I will stay as long as Allah SWT has willed that I stay in that state". Meaning it will be for a time frame that even the Prophet SAW doesn't even have words for.

Then the Prophet SAW said a beautiful phrase, "Allah SWT will tach me a way to praise him, that I don't know right now". Meaning, he knows what's going to happen, but he doesn't know the details of what's going to happen. He knows that it is his job that he has to do Sajda in front of Allah SWT. He knows that he's going to stay there for a long time. He knows Allah SWT will teach him something. But he doesn't know what it will be.

Prophet SAW continues, "Then when I say that special phrase, Allah SWT will say 'Ya Muhammad SAW raise up your head now. You can raise up. Ask you shall be given. Here you should be spoken. Intercede your intercession will be accepted'."

Then the hadith goes on, "Then I will intercede. And Allah SWT will allow me to intercede. And he will tell me who to intercede for. And I will intercede for them. And

Allah SWT will accept their intercession. I will then continue to come back to Allah SWT, and I will continue to intercede until no one remains in Jahannam except those whom the Quran has given permanent Jahannam to".

Meaning the Mushrikun. Those that did not believe in Allah SWT. The Prophet SAW then added in the same Hadith that, "Whoever has an atom's weight of Iman they will be removed from the fire of hell".

In another version of the Hadith, he said, "Whoever says La Ilaha Ill Allah, and has a mustard's grain of Iman shall be removed from the fire of hell. Until none shall remain except those that have absolutely no Iman".

Now Maqam Al Mahmood or grand Shafa'a, in this case, is by him prostration and making dua to Allah SWT to begin the judgment day. The beginning of judgment is what mankind wanted.

However, the very next phrases that mention the Shafa'a of the Prophet SAW for his Ummah. That is not Maqam Al Mahmood. The Scholars have said that it appears to be the case that the narrators are condensing 2 different incidents in one Hadith. Or the Prophet SAW himself is narrating one incident and then another incident, that are not necessarily causally linked together.

The first Shafa'a is Maqam Al Mahmood and the second Shafa'a is the Shafa'a for his Ummah. For those who say La Ilaha Ill Allah. These are two separate Shafa'a. Also, the narration seems to propose that both events are continuous and chronological. But they are not.

Maqam Al Mahmood is for all of mankind, with no restriction. That's why it's the highest level. There's no concept of forgiveness in this Shafa'a. That's just to begin judgement day.

Shafa'a for Those Decreed to Jahannam

Now the rest of these Shafa'a are not in chronological order. They will occur at different times, throughout the day of judgement. They're not all occurring at the beginning. The only one that's occurring at the beginning is the Maqam Al Mahmood. And Shafa'a is an ongoing process, from Maqam Al Mahmood, up until even after the believers enter Jannah and they are in Jannah and they are enjoying the fruits of Jannah.

The Second Category of Shafa'a is for those whom the decree has been given that they're going to Jahannam. They've been handed the registrars. They've been handed the verdicts in the left hand. They know they're going to Jahannam. They've been chained up on the plains of Judgment day.

But, instead of being dragged to Jahannam, Shafa'a will come and they will not go to Jahannam. They shall be forgiven and they shall enter Jannah without going to Jahannam. Even though the verdict was given.

Imam Al Nawawi RA said, "Another type of Shafa'a in for those for whom Jahannam has been decreed. But the Prophet SAW will make Shafa'a and Allah SWT will cause them to go to Jannah". Al Qurtubi RA said the same thing. Al Qa'deyat RA said the same thing. Ibn Hajar RA said the same thing.

Ibn Al Qayyim RA comes along and he says, "I searched for any evidence for this type of Shafa'a. And up until writing these lines, I could not find any Hadith that mentions this category explicitly. I couldn't find something that is very explicit. That before going to Jahannam, people are taken away and taken to Jannah".

Some later Scholars have found certain writings of the Sahaba in weak traditions, that explicitly talk about people who on the day of judgment are pulled aside and instead of going to Jahannam, they go to Jannah. But their chains of narrations are not authentic.

So, we can make a clause that as far as we know, there's no explicit authentic Hadith for this type of Shafa'a. There are implied Hadith that Shafa'a is taking place. So, we do not know for certain. But it makes sense that this Shafa'a exist. But many Scholars have affirmed this concept and it makes sense that some people will not go to Jahannam.

Shafa'a for the Major Sinner in Jahannam

The third category is the most obvious and the most well-documented category of Shafa'a. This is the Shafa'a for the major sinner who are in Jahannam. That they be removed from Jahannam before their time is up. This is the largest category of Shafa'a. It is general for anyone whom Allah SWT wishes. Not only for our Prophet SAW. Anyone whom Allah wishes can get this Shafa'a.

Every righteous person to person who's going to Jannah, might be given the right to ask Allah SWT and then it is up to Allah SWT to accept. Allah SWT may give them permission to ask. After you have asked, Allah SWT is going to be the one who decides.

So Shafa'a for the major sinners of this Ummah, the ones who are in Jahannam, they are inside Jahannam, but then the are removed before their time is up. Obviously, this is not happening on the day of judgment chronologically. This is happening afterwards.

Now this category is affirmed in Sunni Islam. Even the Quran indirectly mentions Shafa'a as linked to people going to Jahannam. And the only reason why Allah SWT would mention Shafa'a after mentioning people going to Jahannam is that some people will not remain in Jahannam, and Shafa'a will come in.

Allah SWT says in the Quran that, "On that day we should gather up the righteous. And we will send them in delegation in front of Ar Rehman. And we shall drag the sinners to Jahannam in hoards upon hordes. None of them will hold any Shafa'a except the one whom Allah SWT has given permission and has a promise to do".

Now, why is Allah SWT mentioning after the sinners, that there are some that the Shafa'a will have an impact? Whomever Allah SWT has allowed; they will have Shafa'a. This indicates that some of the sinners, the Shafa'a of the people for them will be accepted by Allah SWT.

From the Hadith we have many evidences. Of them is the Hadith of Jabir Ibn Abdullah RA, which is simple, sweet and to the point. You cannot get more explicit and more to the point than this. Prophet SAW said, "The purpose of my Shafa'a is for the major sinner of Ummah".

Our Scholars mention, of what use is Shafa'a for the one who prays tahajud and is Muttaqi? He doesn't need the Shafa'a. The concept of Shafa'a is for the sinful Muslims, who didn't do enough good. They believed in the Prophet SAW and the Prophet SAW will then make Shafa'a for them.

Who are the sinners? The drug addicts, the drunkards, the ones who committed Zina, those who didn't pray regularly. These are the major sinners. They are being punished and they need Shafa'a.

In another Hadith of the Prophet SAW, He said, "There will be groups of people in Jahannam, who will be caused to leave because of my Shafa'a". This is after day of judgment. Hisab been done. People are in Jannah and Jahannam. Then there will be groups of people that will be taken out because of this Shafa'a of Prophet SAW.

What does it mean that they're going to be taken out? It means before their time was up. If they got five hundred years, then maybe in 100 years they'll be let go.

The Prophet SAW said, "It will be said to them these are people from Jahannam". Meaning people of Jannah will call them by this title for a certain period of time.

This Shafa'a is not only for our Prophet SAW. It is for all the righteous, the Hafiz, the Ulema, the Martyrs, and even for the Angels. The Angels who loved some person because they used to read Quran or do Zikr etc.; they will make Shafa'a for them.

Therefore, we should never trivialize the opportunity to do any good. We don't know what Angel is there. We don't know one sadaqa, one good deed, one smile might get us Shafa'a. We don't know what's going to happen. We learn from the traditions that the people of Jannah will have perfect memories. They will remember a person who was good to them, or helped them when they needed help.

They will remember whenever Allah SWT wants them to remember. When they will realize that person is not in Jannah. They will ask the Angels, and they will be told that this person is in Jahannam. And it is possible, if Allah SWT wills, that they will make Shafa'a for that person, and it is possible that Shafa'a will be accepted.

In Musnad Imam Ahmed, Abubakar Sadiq RA narrated that, "Allah SWT will say to the Angels on the day of judgement, call the righteous for me. Then the righteous people will be brought to Allah SWT. Then Allah SWT will ask them to make Shafa'a, and they will Shafa'a. Then Allah SWT ask Angels to bring the Martyrs. Then the Martyrs will come. Martyrs will be asked to make Shafa'a, and they will make Shafa'a".

In another Narration, "Allah SWT will call the Prophets AS, they will be called to make Shafa'a". Then the rest of the hadith is the same as above.

In the famous Hadith of Saeed Al Khudri RA, which is in Bukhari and Muslim, where the Prophet SAW mentioned that, "Batches of people will pass over the Sirat. Some are going to go at the speed of light. Some are going to go at the speed of a galloping horse. Some will go at the speed of a fast man. Some at speed of a slow man. Some are going to go walking. Some will go crawling. Until finally the last one of them is dragging over the Sirat. Until when they have crossed over the Sirat, and they see that they have passed and they are certain that they've passed over, and are essentially movements away from gates of Jannah, and they still haven't entered Jinnah; they will turn to Allah SWT and they will say to Allah SWT, 'Our Lord our brothers the ones who fell down from the Sirat, and they weren't able to cross over, these people would pray with us. They would fast with us. They would do good deeds with us. We know them. Please Forgive them'."

Meaning people who crossed the Sirat will be begging to Allah SWT as they are one step away from Jannah. If they wanted to, they could have turned their backs on their brother and walked away. But these are their families and their relatives. The people that they would pray with and do good deeds with. So, they have in their hearts the Iman that brings about that brotherhood.

The Prophet SAW continued, and this is human nature, "Once they know they are safe, then they will turn to Allah SWT for their loved ones. Before that it is Nafsi-Nafsi. And they will be the most argumentative as possible in front of Allah SWT of to save their brothers".

Subhan Allah! Now that they are certain that they got in, there is no chance of them going back, they going to be arguing to Allah SWT in a positive way, for the people that didn't make it, by pointing out their good deeds. This is happening right outside of Jannah. This is them making Shafa'a.

So, Allah SWT will say to whomever he pleases, "Go. Whoever you find, who has a Dinar's weight of Iman, then go and get them out". The Prophet SAW has said that Allah SWT has made Jahannam Haram upon the place that you do sajda. Where do we do Sajda? The face and the hands and the feet. How do you recognize somebody? By the face.

This is a very interesting phrase, that the Prophet SAW is indicating that the rest of the people are unrecognizable. So somehow the people who are destined to go to Jannah have the capability to tour Jahannam as if they are not in Jahannam. They're walking around and they're not in it. And they're searching for their family, their friends, their relatives, those who did good deeds with them, and have a dinar's worth of Iman.

Now, Allah SWT will allow them to see various people and they will be able to recognize the people who have more than a dinner's Iman. Then they will be allowed to be taken out. That will be the first batch.

Then they will ask Allah SWT one more time. Allah SWT will say, "Go and find somebody who has half a Dinar's weight of Iman and take him out". Now notice more time has passed by, which means more punishment has been given to people with Half a Dinar's weight in Iman. So, people with Iman of Half a Dinar will be taken out.

Then people will ask Allah SWT again, and process will keep on repeating, until finally Allah SWT will say, "Whoever has the smallest bit of an atom's weight of Iman, take him out". So those people will be taken out.

Then Allah SWT will say, "The Prophets AS have given their Shafa'a. The Malaika have given their Shafa'a. The believers have given their Shafa'a. And no one is left except The Most Merciful".

Now, when is this happening? According to one Hadith it appears that this is happening on the day of judgement. However, it is not incorrect to understand that this type of Shafa'a begins from the day of judgement and it lasts for as long as Allah SWT wants it to last. It is possible that somebody from Jannah will recognize or remember someone. And they will be allowed to look down who is there and take that person out.

So, eons will go by. Because obviously not everybody will be taken out of Jahannam on the day of judgement. Clearly, this is common sense.

We learn this from other Hadiths that, the Prophet SAW said, "The dweller of hell will actually be told to enter

Jannah, and by that time everybody in Jannah will be settled. Then the former dwellers of Jahannam will say to Allah SWT that there is no space left. Everybody is at ease now. Then Allah SWT will expand Jannah, and space will be made for them. Then they're going to be let in".

This is not happening on the day of judgement. The point being that this notion of people coming in and taking people out, even though in one hadith it might appear that it is all happening on the day of judgment, in reality we need to understand that this is an ongoing process. It begins on the day of judgement and it will last until the last person of Jahannam has been removed.

Then Allah SWT will say, "No one is remaining except for me, the Jabbar and Arhamur Rahimin. And no one's Shafa'a is left except for my Shafa'a." The Prophet SAW continues that, "Then Allah SWT will lift a hand full from Jahannam". And a handful of Allah SWT is many people. We cannot even imagine such a large handful.

It will be the last batch that no previous group of people even recognized. And the Prophet SAW said, "These will be the people that have never done any good deed". Now Scholars have discussed the meaning of "never done any good deed". Some have argued if it means literally no good deed or is this a figure of speech.

Where what the Prophet SAW meant to say is very few good deeds.

The Prophet SAW continues, "Allah SWT will take them out. They will be been scarred and completely disfigured. Allah SWT will tell them to jump into the river. They will jump into the river, and they will come out fully pure and fully whole again. Then they will be told to enter Jannah". This is the third category of Shafa'a for the people that are the major sinners that have entered Jahannam.

Those to Enter Jannah Without Hisab

The fourth category of Shafa'a on the day of judgment is that, there will be a small group of people who shall enter Jannah without any Hisab or accounting. That group of people, they are the elite of this Ummah. Because the bulk of this Ummah, they will undergo Hisab.

That group, how do they get there? One batch of them will get there because of the Shafa'a of the Prophet SAW. But most of them will get there because of their good deeds.

The most famous evidence for this is a famous Hadith of Ukasha RA, that that has become an expression in Arabic. This famous Hadith of Imran Ibn Al Hussain RA states that our Prophet SAW mentioned that, "There's going to be a large group of people on the day of judgement. I will see that these are my Ummah. Then Jibreel AS will tell me that of this large group, 70000 will enter Jannah without Hisab".

So, someone asked the Prophet SAW, "Who are these 70,000 people?" The Prophet SAW said, "They are those who they do not ask others to do Ruqya on them. And they do not believe in Omens. And they do not practice that type of medicine in which burning was done. And they put their trust in Allah SWT".

Now, what combines all of these characteristics is there belief in Allah SWT is perfect. A man stood up, and his name was Ukasha RA, and said, "Am I from amongst them O Messenger of Allah SAW?" The Prophet SAW said, "Yes you are". Another man stood up and said, "Am I amongst them?" And the Prophet SAW said, "Ukasha preceded you".

Now this Hadith does not explicitly mention that the Prophet SAW did Shafa'a for Ukasha RA. It simply says, "You are amongst them". And Ukasha RA was a famous Sahabi. He was in Battle of Badr and Battle of Uhud. He died fighting the Murtad during the time of Abu Bakr Siddiq RA.

He was the one who in the Battle of Uhud, when his sword broke up, Prophet SAW handed him a branch and he SAW said, "Go fight with this". Ukasha RA took the branch, and he turned to face the enemy, and he raised his hand, and Allah SWT converted it into a sword in his hand.

Now, there's another wording of this Hadith in Sahih Muslim that Ukasha RA stood up and said, "Ya Rasool Allah SAW make Dua that I am amongst those 70,000". And Prophet SAW said "Yes you are". This is the Shafa'a here. So, this is a very explicit Hadith.

Now 70,000 is a very small number compared to the size of Ummah. Good news is that in Musnad Imam Ahmed, narrated from Abu Bakr Siddique RA, Prophet SAW said, "I have been gifted 70000 of my Ummah that shall enter Jannah without Hisab. Their faces are as bright as the full moon in the middle of the month. And their hearts are all pure. But then I asked Allah SWT for more than 70,000. Then Allah SWT gifted me for every one person from the original batch, there shall be another 70,000".

This shows us the mercy that our Prophet SAW had, that Allah SWT gifted him. Because he doesn't need this gift. But he loves the Ummah so much that he asked for more. Realize that 70000 by 70000 is 4.9 billion. Now is that 4.9 billion enough? How many Muslims are in right now? Roughly between 1.5 Billion to 2 Billion. And in last slightly over 1440 years, how many Muslims have there been? Therefore, from that math 4.9 billion is a very good number to cover almost the entire Ummah up till this point in time.

Now, there's another version of this Hadith in Tirmidhi, Prophet SAW said, "I asked Allah SWT for more and so for every 1000 of the original, Allah SWT gave me another 70000". So, this way the number comes down to 4.9 million. And Allah SWT knows best. We hope it is 4.9 billion. Inshallah!

General Shafa'a

The next category of Shafa'a is what is called the general or generic Shafa'a for everybody. This Shafa'a is the Shafa'a that no one from the Ummah of the Prophet SAW will remain in Jahannam. No one who believed in the Prophet SAW shall remain in Jahannam permanently. This is a generic Shafa'a.

There's one Hadith that every Muslim needs to know, and think about, and appreciate and thank Allah SWT for, and then send Salawat on the prophet SAW. There is one Hadith that really deserves that we actually make this a separate category. Hadith is in Sahih Muslim and is authentic.

The Prophet SAW said, "Every single Nabi was given one dua that Allah SWT guaranteed that Allah SWT will give him. And Every Nabi used his dua in this Dunya. As for me, I have held on to my Dua. I have kept it to myself and I will use it on the day of judgment as a Shafa'a for my Ummah. Any one that dies with La Ilaha Ill Allah, anyone who dies without committing Shirk, will get that Shafa'a".

So, this Shafa'a is for every single believer in our Prophet SAW. It shows us the sacrifice that our Prophet SAW did. He could have used this dua for so many things. He could have used this at Uhud, at Badr, at Tabuk, or he could have used it for his uncle Abu Talib.

He could have used this dua at any junction of his life, but he kept it. So that with this one dua, Allah SWT will eventually forgive the entire Ummah.

Shafa'a to Open Gates of Jannah

The sixth category is Shafa'a to enter through the gates of Jannah. It is the Shafa'a to open the gates of Jannah. It is the Shafa'a for the people of Jannah to enter Jannah. No one will enter Jannah up until the Prophet SAW is the one who knocks on the doors of Jannah.

The first person to knock on the doors of Jannah will be the Prophet SAW. He will be the one whom the Angels will open the door for. So, this is the Shafa'a, the asking for opening the gates of Jannah.

In the Hadith in Bukhari that, Allah SWT will say to the Prophet SAW that, "Take this group of people and enter Jannah from the right door and only this group will enter from the right door. Then the rest of your Ummah will share with the rest of the Ummahs all the other door".

In other words, there is a special door of Jannah, that will be the first go to open. Our Prophet SAW well be opening that door and the people who will be entering Jannah without any Hisab, they will enter through that door. This is a category of Shafa'a that is only for our Prophet SAW.

Shafa'a for The People of Medina

Number seven is the Shafa'a for the people of Medina. This is a special category of Shafa'a that only our Prophet SAW has it.

Hadith is in Bukhari that, "Medina is a blessed city. Medina is the sacred city between these two planes of rock. Whoever is patient at the problems of Medina and the trials of Medina, the diseases in Medina, and whoever is patient with the trails of Medina, and the issues of Medina; then I shall do Shafa'a for him on the day of Judgment".

And in the Hadith of Tirmidhi, the Prophet SAW said, "Whoever amongst you is able to die in the city of Medina, let him die in the city of Medina. Because whoever dies in Medina, I will make Shafa'a for him".

So, we ask Allah SWT for a death in Medina and to be buried in Al-Baqi. As it is a great honor. Our Prophet SAW has made a special dua and special Shafa'a for him. In fact, it was the last thing that he did when he was healthy. In the middle of the night Jibreel AS asked him to go to Al-Baqi.

So, he walked in the middle of the night to Al-Baqi, and he made dua for them and he came home and he fell sick and he passed away because of that sickness. So, the people of Medina are blessed. Those who live there and those who died there and those who are Buried there. So, whenever you go to Medina, that should be our dua to ask Allah SWT for a death in Medina.

Umar Ibn Al-Khattab RA famously said, "I want to die in Medina and I want to die a Shaheed". His son said, "O my father, you can't combine between the two. To die a Shaheed would mean dying while fighting outside of Medina". He said, "Allah SWT is capable of everything". And Umar RA died in as a Shaheed in Medina.

Shafa'a to Raise Status of People of Jannah

Category number eight is the Shafa'a to raise the status of the people of Jannah to a higher level of Jannah. This is a very simple category, that we all understand. This is somebody who got in on a lower level of Jannah, but a loved one made Shafa'a and he got to the same level of Jannah as that Loved one.

This is a very common category. Now, some of our Scholars have said that this is the default of every person in Jannah. That if you make it to Jannah, you can make Shafa'a for those with in Jannah to be raised to a level with you if you want them to be there.

Our Prophet SAW said, "Whoever you love you will be with that person in Jannah". So, this is a Shafa'a that everyone has. The Prophet SAW has it. The righteous have it. However, there's nothing explicit about this. But the concept in found.

Allah SWT says, "Them and their wives will be together in Jannah". At another place Allah SWT says, "Those that were good and their children were good, we will allow the children to be with them in Jannah".

How else is that going to happen, except through the category of Shafa'a. There is evidence for this in a beautiful Hadith in Musnad Imam Ahmed and also there's a version of it in Bukhari, where the prophet SAW said when somebody passed away. His name was Abu Salama RA. The prophet SAW made due for that person for raising his ranks.

Shafa'a for Abu Talib

Number 9, the final category, that is unique to our Prophet SAW. It is Shafa'a for his uncle Abu Talib. Ibn Abbas RA said to Prophet SAW, "Ya Rasool Allah SAW, your uncle Abu Talib, he's really did a lot for you and he protected you and he took so much on for you. Were you able to benefit him in any way?"

It is because Abu Talib died a non-Muslim. The Prophet SAW said, "Yes. I made Shafa'a for him, and because of that, Allah SWT has taken him out from the very depths of Jahannam, and moved him to the corner regions which are not as intense. If it were not for my Shafa'a, he would have remained in the depts of Jahannam."

Scholars say that this Shafa'a is unique because no other human, no other Muslim, no other Angel can make Shafa'a for a Kafir. But our Prophet SAW was allowed to make a partial Shafa'a, and that Shafa'a was not enough to get him outside of Jahannam. Because in the end he did not worship Allah SWT.

If you don't worship Allah SWT then there is no hope. He rejected Islam knowing what Islam was. But for our Prophet SAW, Abu Talib was not a normal regular Kafir. He took on so much pressure, and he remained firm up on Justice, and he stood up for the truth, and he sacrificed his ego, and his reputation for the sake of the one person, who is the most precious in all of mankind. That person is his nephew the Prophet SAW.

So, because he took care of the Prophet SAW that helped him partially. Because of that partial Shafa'a he is now in the very corner of Jahannam. Otherwise he would be in the very depths of Jahannam.

How to Get Shafa'a of Prophet SAW

We now move on to what are the actions that can help us to get the Shifa of the Prophets SAW. What are the things that are mentioned in the Sunnah that can increase our chances for obtaining that Shafa'a? A number of things are mentioned.

Number one on this list the most important thing to get Shafa'a of our Prophet SAW is, as he SAW said, "When you hear the Moazin, repeat after him and then send your salat upon me and then ask Allah SWT to grant me the Wasilla. Sor whoever asks Allah SWT for Waseela for me, my Shafa'a will become halal for him".

This hadith is in Sahih Muslim and versions of it are found in Bukhari and others. So, we have over here one of the most explicit linkage between doing something and getting Shafa'a. Now, what is the Wasilla? There is a hadith in Musnad Imam Ahmed that our Prophet SAW said, "Waseela is a level of Jannah. There is no level higher than this level. So, ask Allah SWT to give me that Wasilla".

Our Prophet SAW said, "Whenever you ask Allah SWT for the Wasilla for me, My Shafa'a becomes halal obligatory upon you. Allah SWT will grant you my Shafa'a". Remember all Shafa'a goes back to Allah SWT.

Even in this phrasing, the Prophet SAW didn't say, "I will give you". He said, "Allah SWT will make it Halal for you to obtain my Shafa'a".

Meaning Allah Azza Wajal will allow you to obtain this Shafa'a. Remember all Shafa'a belong to Allah Subhanahu WA Ta'ala.

Number two, some Ulama have derived from this hadith that sending salat upon the Prophet SAW also grants us the Shafa'a. Because the hadith says, when you hear the Adhan, say what Moazin says. Then send your salat upon the Prophet SAW. Then ask for Wasilla. Whoever does so will get his Shafa'a. Two things are mentioned actually.

Therefore, some of our scholars have derived that sending salawat wat upon the Prophet SAW and making it something that is constant. Therefore, the one who constantly sends salawat upon our Rasool SAW, then the possibility of that person getting Prophet SAW's Shafa'a are higher.

Number three, of the ways we can increase the chances of getting the Shafa'a of the Prophet SAW for us is, as Abu Huraira RA said, "Ya Rasool Allah who will be the luckiest person or the one who has the lion's share of your Shafa'a on the day of judgment? Who has the most chances of getting your Shafa'a on day of judgment?"

This is a very explicit hadith, where Abu Huraira is asking our Prophet SAW. Hadith is in Muslim. The Prophet SAW responded, "I thought that nobody would ask me this question before you, o Abu Huraira because of your eagerness. The one who has the most chance for my Shafa'a on the day of judgement is the one who says La Ilaha Ill Allah sincerely from his heart".

So, to get the Shafa'a we should perfect our Tauheed. Saying the Kalema from our heart, and implementing it, and acting upon it in our lives. Especially the one who says the Kalema at the time of death. Even though that is not linked to the Shafa'a, but we know from other traditions that the one who says La Ilaha Illallah constantly, and inshallah the one who says at the time of death, has a higher chance of getting the Shafa'a.

In fact, according to this hadith, we should put this number one, not number three. But all of these are valid points. Because the hadith says who has the most chance, who has the luckiest opportunity. That person going to be the happiest.

Point number four about what will grant us the Shafa'a of the Prophet SAW, we can say that it is making lots of salawat and especially Sajdas. From this we can also make Qiyas analogy, about doing lots of good deeds.

There is a beautiful tradition in Musnad Imam Ahmed that one day, one of the servants of the Prophet SAW was doing Khidmah to him, and the Prophet says said to him, "What can I give you back?" Meaning do you want a horse? Do you want to camel? You want some money? How can I help you back?

Also, a point to be made here, in the Seerah of the SAW, every single slave that he was gifted, he eventually freed every single one of them. According to some reports of from Ibn Sa'd RA and others, they mention that the Prophet SAW was given over 30 slaves by the dignitaries and delegations that would come. Or the Sahaba would gift him.

Slavery was well known back then. And he freed every one of them. He did not have a male slave that was a Khadim. But when he freed them, many of them volunteered to be his servants. They remained with him to give him Khidmah.

This was a common theme throughout his life, that he would have many free people who volunteered to become his servant. Anas Ibn Malik RA is one of the examples, that his mother gifted him to Prophet SAW, and Anas RA became Khadim of Nabi SAW.

Same way, we have one of these servants, that one day the Prophet SAW said, "What can I give you back?" Meaning in the concept of this dunya. The man said, "What do I want? I want your Shafa'a on the day of judgment". The Prophet said, "Who told you to ask me this? Did someone advised you to ask this?" Meaning Prophet SAW wasn't expecting him to ask for a Shafa'a. The servant said, "Allah SWT put it in my heart".

The Prophet SAW said that, "If that is what you want, help me to get your request". Notice he could not guarantee. That is Allah SWT and only Allah SWT. Even the Nabi SAW does not have the power to cause somebody to enter Jannah.

Now what can he do to help get the Shafa'a? prophet SAW said, "Do lots and lots of sujood and Salawats. Pray a lot and I'll try to get my Shafa'a to you". From this we extrapolate that the one who comes with lots of good deeds on the day of Judgment has more of a chance of the Shafa'a of the Prophet SAW.

These are the four authentic things that are mentioned in the books of hadith. There are others that are not authentic but are well known. We'll mention one of them. This is mentioned in a number of traditions at least four or five. But all of them are weak or very weak or even very clearly fabricated.

It is that visiting the resting place of the Prophet SAW bring about the Shafa'a of the Prophet SAW. Perhaps the most well-known Hadith of them, even though it is clearly weak, is that Prophet SAW said, "Whoever visits my grave my Shafa'a will become Waajib upon him".

Who Can Give Shafa'a?

Who else can give Shafa'a? We gave many categories about the types of Shafa'a of the Prophet SAW, and how some of them apply to other people as well. Now, we need to mention who else will give Shafa'a.

Prophets AS

Number one, other Prophets AS will give Shafa'a. This is commonly understood. There are many hadith in this regard that Shafa'a is open to all the Prophets AS. The Prophets AS will make Shafa'a for their own nations. This is something that is understood, it is logical and it is textual.

Of the many evidences for this, is the hadith of Bukhari that was quoted in previous chapters that at the very end when all of the people have interceded, Allah SWT will say, "The Angels have made their Shafa'a, the Prophets AS have made their Shafa'a, the Shaheed have made their Shafa'a, the righteous have made their Shafa'a. No one is left except for me. Now I will make my Shafa'a".

This clearly shows that the Prophets AS will do Shafa'a. As well, we have the famous hadith in Musnad Imam Ahmed that, "On the day of judgement, the Prophets AS will be standing on the Sirat, and they will be making dua for their Ummah as they cross the Sirat. The Prophets will therefore be making Shafa'a for their Ummah as they cross the Sirat".

So, each Prophet AS will be monitoring their own flock. Each Prophet will be asking Allah SWT for protection for its own followers. So, the Prophets AS all of them have the power of Shafa'a. Allah SWT has blessed them with it. However, the quantity and the quality of the Shafa'a of the Prophet SAW is beyond that of all of the other Prophets AS, and we thank Allah SWT for being in the Ummah of the Prophet SAW.

The Angels

Category 2 are the Angels who have the right of Shafa'a. Again, this is very clear from hadith. In fact, there are explicit verses in the Quran that affirm that the Angels are going to make Shafa'a for the believers. Allah SWT says, "The Angels will only make Shafa'a for those whom Allah SWT is pleased with".

Another evidence from the Quran which is the most explicit verse in the Quran where Allah SWT says, "How many are the Angels? Beyond count. You will never know O mankind. How many are the Angels that they are making Shafa'a in the heavens. But there Shafa'a is of no use. Except for those whom Allah SWT has allowed".

Now this means the Angels are making Shafa'a and it's up to Allah SWT who he accepts or doesn't. As Shafa'a is simply a mechanism that Allah SWT uses to forgive people. But Angels have been given the right to ask Allah SWT for Shafa'a for people. This Ayah is from Surah Najam.

There's one other Ayah that is in Surah Ghafir, verse 7 to 8. Allah SWT says, "The Angels that are carrying the throne and the Angels around them, they are praising Allah SWT. They are believing in Allah SWT. And they are asking forgiveness for the believers".

This is an explicit affirmation that the Angels, and not just any Angels, the angels that are at the peak; the ones carrying the throne, and the Angels all around them, are asking Allah SWT's forgiveness for the righteous and for the believers. They're begging Allah SWT to protect the believers. This is Shafa'a. They're asking Allah SWT to cause us to enter Jannah, and our children, and our parents.

They're asking Allah SWT to protect us on the day of judgement. All of this is Shafa'a. Which is explicitly affirmed in the Quran that the Angels are asking Shafa'a for the believers.

We also learned this in a number of hadiths. Other than the one that we mentioned in the beginning of this chapter, there is another hadith that says, "The Angels they want to record the good deeds, and they want to report to Allah SWT. The purpose of reporting those good deeds to Allah SWT and the purpose of being around the righteous is none other than to make Shafa'a for them".

It is authentically narrated that once a Sahabi was reciting Surah Al-Isra and Surah Al-Kahf and he saw a light like a chandelier come down. Every time he recited; it came down. When he stopped reciting, it went up. He asked the Prophet SAW about this. The Prophet SAW said, "This is the Angels that came down to listen to your recitation".

The Angels love piety. They love righteousness. They love Taqwa and manifestations of Taqwa. When we recite the Quran or do Zikr, the Angels surround us. The Angels surround the circles of knowledge. So much so that the Prophet SAW said, "The Angels will pile up and gather all the way to the heavens to be around the people who have gathered together to remember Allah Subhana WA Ta'ala".

In the hadith in Abu Dawood is says that a man made a beautiful Dua and Zikr, and the Prophet SAW came and asked, "Who was the one who said this phrase of dua and Zikr? For by Allah SWT he said something good". A Sahaba stood up said, "I am the one who said it Ya Rasool Allah SAW". The Prophets SAW said, "I saw over 30 Angels racing back to Allah SWT to see who could be the first to tell Allah SWT of what you have said".

What is the purpose of the Angel racing back? It's to make the Shafa'a. The point is that the Angels love Taqwa and Iman. And it is possible that an Angel likes a person for their good deeds. An angel sees this person has helped out somebody. This person has helped a poor person in secret. This person has prayed Tahajud. Angels are sentient beings. They are smart being. They're intelligent beings. The Angels have thoughts like we do.

So, it is possible that the Angel likes a person for their good deeds, and so they will then ask Allah Azza WA Jal that to forgive a person because he would read Quran, or a person would pray tahajud. Therefore, the Angels are also a group that will intercede and will make Shafa'a to Allah SWT on the day of judgment. So, we should do good deeds as Angels are all around us recoding them.

The Shuhada

Category 3 is the Shahada or the Martyrs. Martyrs have a special category, because they are mentioned in the hadith. Our Prophet SAW said, "The martyrs have six blessings that no one else does. Of them is that every Shaheed has 70 people that he can make Shafa'a for, from the people around him". This doesn't include his family. It can mean his friends and colleagues and associates.

So, the Shaheed has 70 people that is a guaranteed quota that he will be allowed to make Shafa'a for. Now, about the categories of Shaheed, the question is that, there is a real Shaheed who dies in battle and then we have the Shaheed in Baraka but not in the same Hukum. Meaning the Shaheed who dies by drowning, or the Shaheed who dies by a natural accident, or by a stomach disease, or the mother who gives birth and dies.

These are all Shaheed in Baraka but not Shaheed in Hukum. They have a different category. This 70 does it apply to the actual Shaheed in the battle or does it apply to any Shaheed?

Ibn Hajar RA discussed this and he comes to the conclusion that it appears that it applies to the actual Shaheed of the battle. That is the one who dies in the

Battle. Others have disagreed and have said that this applies to everybody.

But the hadith is very clear that the Shaheed has six things. Number one is that, "As soon as the sword strikes him, his sins are forgiven". It's very explicit on which category of Shaheed it is talking about. That is the Shaheed that dies in the battle. That Shaheed has 70 people that he shall intercede for.

The Righteous People

Category 4 is what we can extrapolate that all righteous people will have ability to make Shafa'a. Now, Shaheed is a righteous person. Or Prophets AS are righteous people. But because it is mentioned specifically that they have a special blessing, they have their own category.

This category is for any common regular person, who is a righteous person. Meaning any Mumin, any Muttaqi, any Siddique, anyone who has Iman and Taqwa. Allah SWT can gift him a quantity. Just like the Shaheed is given 70. Allah can gift a person one, or two, or ten, or fifteen, or twenty, or seven hundred.

Remember of the gifts of the believer who passes over the Sirat, who passes everything, that they will be given a quota. At times it can be ambiguous. Meaning not specifying a number but rather a condition. Like having Iman of the size of an Atom. This quota is a sign of Allah SWT's pleasure for this person. It does not mean that it's a get out of jail free card.

It is a tipping of the scales. Then it's up to Allah SWT. It is one extra perk, then is up to Allah Azza Wajal. In the end Shafa'a is a mechanism through which Allah SWT honors one group of people by giving them ability to make Shafa'a and uses those people to forgive another group of people that he wanted to forgive anyway.

Now who will they choose? People that they knew in this dunya. Their extended family, friends and people they owe favor to. They are going to choose the ones that were righteous and good to them.

This is actually authentically mentioned about, for example we mentioned earlier about the one who would give loans and he would not take it back and would say, "I am a sinner. I'll forgive them, Allah SWT will forgive me". May be this person for this good deed, gets forgiven and gets to make Shafa'a. Or someone whose loan he let go gets to make Shafa'a for him.

Now there are a number of explicit hadith. Most of them are slightly weak. But some of them are definitely authentic. Of the authentic ones, we mentioned previously, is the hadith of the Sirat. That our Prophet SAW said, "Once people cross over the Sirat, and they've now made it, those Muslims who have crossed over the Sirat, they will be the most pleading in front of Allah Subhana wa Ta'ala in their case for their brethren who didn't cross over the Sirat".

They will say, "O Allah these are our brothers. We prayed together. We fasted together. We gave zakat together. Save them with us". So, they're now making Shafa'a to Allah Subhana wa Ta'ala. The hadith says, Allah SWT will allow a group of people to save whomever they want. They will be given a quota. Even that will be in batches as we explained earlier.

Another hadith from Tirmidhi, which is slightly weak, we learn that, "The Hafiz of Quran will come on the day of judgment and his two parents will have crowns made out of light". In another narration, which is also weak, it says that, "the Hafiz will have ten Shafa'a".

In Sunnah Ibn Maja, in a hadith with slight weakness, our Prophet SAW said, "Three shall intercede on the day of judgment. The Prophets and the then the Ulema and then the Shaheed". So, the Ulema have been put here in this hadith in the category of the righteous people.

All of this can be put together to say every single believer has the potential for Shafa'a if Allah SWT gives him. The more righteous the Mumin, is the more chances that Shafa'a will be allowed to him.

We also have a number of narrations that even in this dunya Shafa'a begins for the believer. In a Hadith in Sahih Muslim, the Prophet SAW said, "Anyone who dies and a group from the ummah, 100 or more pray for him and make Shafa'a for him, Allah SWT will accept their Shafa'a".

Meaning for the Janazah Salah we should have large quantities. That is why it is a Sunnah to come to Janazah. Whenever somebody passes away, we should make it a point to go to their Janazah. So that when it's our turn, Allah SWT will bless us to have a large Janazah. This hadith mentions 100. Another hadith in Tirmidhi mentions 40. The point is that if there's a large group of people asking for Shafa'a for a person that has passed away, they shall be forgiven.

In another hadith as well in Tirmidhi, our Prophet SAW said, "From my Ummah there shall be groups of people that Allah SWT will bless to make Shafa'a for crowds of people. And others will make Shafa'a for a whole tribe of people. and others will make Shafa'a for a group of people. And there will also be those who make Shafa'a for one person as well".

So, this hadith is very explicit that people have different quantities of Shafa'a. Some people will be given an entire tribe or few thousand. Some people will be given 50 to 100. Some will get 10 to 15. Some people will 1.

In another hadith of Tirmidhi, the Prophet SAW said, "There shall be one man from my Ummah who will be given more Shafa'a than the whole people from the tribe of Banu Tamim". Sahaba asked, "This man is other than you Ya Rasool Allah SAW?" He said, "Yes. This man is other than me".

Now Banu Tamim was the largest Arab tribe back then and it is still the largest tribe today. The tribe of Banu Tamim, it is a massive tribe that still has branches in Iraq and branches in Arabia and branches across the Arab world. And back then the Sahaba were astonished that one man will get to make this many Shafa'a. Imagine in the last 14 centuries how much more that number has increased. One man will be given opportunity to make Shafa'a for millions of people. This is authentically mentioned.

Now, the question arises that can a person ask another person in this dunya, who is a good Muslim, to make Shafa'a from him in Akhira if the opportunity presented itself? Is this request permissible or not? Allah knows best.

But there are a number of evidences that point that it is permissible. There's an indirect evidence and this is reported in the tafseer of Al-Baghawi RA, from Jabir Ibn Abdullah RA that the Prophet SAW said, "There will be a person in Jannah who will remember his friend, and he will say where is my friend. And his friend is in Jahannam. So, Allah Subhana wa Ta'ala will allow him to take his friend out of Jahannam, and cause him to enter in Jannah".

Then he gives the tafseer of the verse in the Quran that Allah SWT says, "And the only people that will be left are those who have no one to intercede. Those who have no loving friends". The tafseer of this verse in the Quran shows that anyone who had a righteous friend and that righteous friend makes it to Jannah, then that righteous friend will be able to make Shafa'a as long as this person himself had Iman.

There is an even more explicit example, that is in Sahih Muslim. It's a very interesting narration. There was a person by name of As-Sunabihi RA. This person wanted to meet the Prophet SAW. He left his land to go meet the Prophet SAW. And he was one of those few unfortunate people that he arrived and the Prophet SAW had just been buried.

He got to Medina literally a few days after the death of the Prophet SAW. He never actually ended up meeting him. He was expecting to arrive in Medina to become a Sahabi. There are at least ten people mentioned by name in the traditions with this case. One of them literally arrived and attended the Janazah of the Prophet SAW. He did not get to see him alive.

So As-Sunabihi RA, he enters the city and he heard the news that the Prophet SAW has passed away. He's not a Sahabi but he is the highest level of the Tabi'un. He prayed behind Abu Bakr Siddique RA. As-Sunabihi RA visited the famous Sahabi Ubadah ibn al-Samit RA on his deathbed. He says, "I saw him lying there and I began to cry seeing him about to pass away". Ubadah ibn al-Samit RA was his teacher and his mentor. Ubadah ibn al-Samit RA said, "Calm down. Why are you crying? For I swear by Allah SWT, if Allah SWT asks me to testify on your behalf, I shall testify on your behalf. And if I am given the right of Shafa'a, I shall make Shafa'a for you".

This is very explicit. Ubadah ibn al-Samit RA is saying this. He is not the Prophet SAW. And he is saying he will help him in any way possible in the Akhira because he's about to die. He is saying this to one of his main students.

Therefore, there is nothing wrong with people saying this to one another. Then Ubadah ibn al-Samit RA says, "There was one hadith I haven't told you and I kept it. Now I'm going to tell it to you because I don't want to die without narrating to you everything I heard".

He said that he heard the Prophet SAW mention, 'Whoever testifies La Ilaha Illallah Muhammad Ur Rasool Allah, the fire of Jahannam is haram for him".

Now, why did Ubadah ibn al-Samit RA and so many Sahaba hesitate to narrate this hadith? This hadith is well known to all of us now. It's in every single book. It is narrated by more than ten Sahaba. But every one of them is hesitant. It is because they fear that the people who hear the hadith will misunderstand it and miss apply it.

They fear that people will just jump on this the hadith and think they don't have to be good they don't have to do rituals. That just believing in La Ilaha Illallah is going to get them in Jannah. Of course, that is not the intent.

Children Who Died in The State of Childhood

Now category number five. Who else has the right of making Shafa'a on the day of judgment? Those children who died in the state of childhood and their parents are patient, they have the Haq of Shafa'a on the day of judgement. And of course, they will make Shafa'a for their parents.

We have many narrations about this. Of them, is the famous hadith in Sahih Muslim, that the Prophet SAW was giving a lecture to the ladies and it is the Sunnah of the Prophet SAW to have regular lectures for the ladies. The Prophet SAW said that, "There is not a single lady amongst you who has three children who died in childhood and she is patient, except that she will enter Jannah".

Now, remember in that time frame the percentage of child mortality was very high. We thank Allah Azza WA Jal that that time is gone. There was a number of academics that did a survey in medieval Europe from 1400 to 1600 about the death rate of children. They estimated around one out of four children died before the age of two and around 40% of children died before the age of fifteen.

Think about that. This is medieval Europe five hundred years ago. In Arabia, 1400 years ago, it would have been even higher than this.

So, a lady stood up and said, "How about if only two died?" The Prophet SAW said, "Even two". From this we can extrapolate that given in our society even one is a bigger deal, because Alhamdulillah the child mortality rate now is less than 1%. This is one of the biggest achievements of modern science across the globe.

So, when a child dies it's a very traumatizing thing for the parents. May Allah SWT protect all of us. Those that have suffered this, we can just imagine, but it is the worst pain that is known to man. There is no pain more difficult than burying your own child. May Allah SWT protect us from that.

So, we can extrapolate that even one from this will be able to get Shafa'a for their parents. In fact, there are evidences of even one. There's a hadith in Sahih Muslim that a man came to Abu Hurairah RA and said that, "I have a child that has died and I want you to tell me something that will calm me down". In another version of this hadith he said, "two children have died".

It's human nature when you go through a tragedy you need some words of encouragement. Abu Huraira RA said that, "Your children are like a baby horse of Jannah. Your child will be spoiled by the love of Jannah. And he shall hold on to your hand (then Abu Huraira RA held on to the hand of this person) like I am holding on to your hand. And he will say, 'I'm not going to let go until I enter Jannah with you'."

Now, the notion of a baby horse is that in Arabian culture it was the most spoiled animal. Wherever it would go, it would get food from people around it and people will pet it and love it. Their heart would be very soft for the baby horse. Because the horse is a prized entity.

Now, Abu Huraira RA is saying this. But he could not have said this from his own mind. He must have obtained this information from the Prophet SAW. And there is a rule in Hadith that when a Shaba says something about that which is considered Ilm Al Ghaib, that saying by default becomes a hadith of Prophet SAW, because the Sahaba would narrate what they heard from him SAW.

There's also a very beautiful hadith in Musnad Imam Ahmed, that the hadith says, "On the day of judgment Angels will come. Then Allah SWT will tell the children to enter Jannah". The children will say, "No. Until our mothers and fathers enter with us". Then they will be asked, "Why are the children angry?"

The children will have a red face, staring with anger. Hadith is describing that the children will be throwing a tantrum. So, Allah will say to the children, "Why are you this angry?" So, they will say, "We want our mothers and fathers. We want them with us. We don't want to be alone in Jannah". So, Allah Subhana WA Ta'ala will say, "Enter Jannah with your mothers and Fathers".

Subhan Allah Ya Arhamur Rahimin! May Allah SWT protect us from ever having to face this tragedy. But for those who have faced this tragedy, they can take this hadith as consolation.

Question comes if this hadith only applies to children who die before the age of puberty or does it apply to any child that dies even if the child was an adult. Our scholars have discussed this, because the Prophet SAW when he is speaking to the women, he says in that hadith "Three children", does that mean it only includes those before puberty.

Both opinions are mentioned by scholars. And Insha'Allah we put our trust in Allah SWT and we expect the best from Allah SWT. We hope the best. Anything that increases our optimism in Allah SWT's Rehma is good.

The Non-Entities

Now, the first five were human beings or Angels. Number six involves things that are beyond entities. They are things beyond beings that can make Shafa'a for us. We know multiple. There are multiple things within this category.

Of them, definitely number one in this list without a doubt is the Quran. Our Prophet SAW said, "Recite the Quran it will come as a Shafa'a for its people on the day of judgment. Its people are those who recited the Quran, and believed in it, and acted upon it, and recited it the way that it deserves to be recited".

Our Prophet said, "The Quran is the one who intercedes and Quran is the one whose intercession is accepted. Quran is the one who argues in front of Allah SWT, and it will be believed by Allah SWT". Here argue means like a defense lawyer arguing that this person shall be forgiven, and the defense lawyer will be believed by Allah SWT.

Quran is an intermediary that will be believed by Allah Subhana WA Ta'ala. This hadith is in Tabarani and is authentic. So, the Quran is very clearly someone who will do Shafa'a for the people.

Our Prophet SAW said, and the hadith is in Bukhara, "It will be said to the Sahib Al Quran to read and recite like used to recite in this dunya. So for every Ayah you read, the Quran will lift you up one Darajat in Jannah. The last ayah you read will be your last place in Jannah".

Also, in the famous hadith as well that our Prophet SAW said, hadith is Musnad Imam Ahmed, "Siam and the Quran will both bring Shafa'a on the day of judgment". The Siam will say, "O Allah I prevented him from food and drink and pleasures in the daytime". The Quran will say, "O Allah I prevented him from sleep at night". The both of them will make Shafa'a and Allah SWT will accept their Shafa'a.

From this we can extrapolate Insha'Allah that all good deeds have the potential to make Shafa'a. It is narrated in some weak hadiths, but the concept is clearly there. That everything that hears the Moazin shall make Shafa'a for him.

The Talbiyah will be a Shafa'a for people. Everything that here's your Talbiyah will make Shafa'a for those people. In other words, things around us and the Quran itself has the potential to make Shafa'a on the day of judgment.

Assalam Waliakum wa Rahmatullahi wa Barakaatuhu,

Brothers and Sisters,

I hope you benefited from this book. If you'd like to read my other books, they are as follows;

1. Dua in Islam
2. Creation in Islam
3. Angels and Jinns in Islam
4. Adam The First Man
5. Guidance from Quran and Sunnah 1, 2 and 3
6. Seerah of Prophet Muhammad SAW 1
7. Jinns and Black Magic
8. The Signs of the Judgement Day
9. The Day of Judgement Part 1 and 2

Jazakallah Khair,

Made in the USA
Las Vegas, NV
19 March 2024